# Soup

By Coralie Castle

Illustrated by Roy Killeen
Published by 101 Productions
San Francisco

Sixth Printing, July, 1976

Distributed to the Book Trade
in the United States of America
by Charles Scribner's Sons, New York

Distributed in Canada by
Van Nostrand Reinhold, Ltd., Scarborough, Ontario

PUBLISHED BY 101 PRODUCTIONS
834 Mission Street, San Francisco, California 94103

Printed in the United States of America
Library of Congress Catalog Card Number 73-174182

# Contents

# Spirit of Soups Past

*"One wit, like a knuckle of ham in the soup, gives zest to the dish, but more than one serves only to spoil the pottage."* —Tobias Smollett

Soup is considered to be the most ancient of foods but its beginning is hard to trace. Archeologists never mention soup, probably because it didn't fossilize, carbonize, desiccate, or leave traces in mummified stomachs.

Just as man was learning to write and record his own history, an ancient Egyptian cook let a bowl of gruel stand too long in the sun, thereby inventing beer. Soon after came mead from honey, wine from grapes, and distilled liquors. Ever since, intrigued writers have been so busy turning out volumes extolling or damning these social beverages, they've had little time or interest left for lowly soup.

Esau, in selling his birthright to Jacob for the pottage of red lentils, was considered a fool. Elisha performed a miracle when he cast meal into a pottage of poisonous boiled wild gourds "and then there was no harm in it." The Israelites made a purée of manna, the secretion of small insects on twigs of the tamarisk, but there is little other biblical reference to soup except when Isaiah wrote, "and broth of abominable things is in their vessels." References to soups show up all over the world. As far back as 2000 B.C., Vedic literature in India mentioned parched barley ground up with juices. Mayan Indians used maize for various liquid foods, most at least mildly alcoholic. Early North American Indians made a broth of hickory-nut milk. Yosemite Indians shredded fungi for mushroom soup and also cooked horse-chestnut gruel. Eskimos still relish fatty soup laced with seal or caribou blood.

## ANCIENT GREECE AND ROME

The Greeks and Romans produced a few historians interested in all kinds of food, including soup. By 600 B.C. in Greece, soups of beans, peas, or lentils relieved the monotony of "bread and a relish," and hot pea soup could be bought in the streets. Kykeon (barley gruel, water, and aromatic herbs like pennyroyal, mint or thyme) served as a ritual beverage at the mysteries of Eleusis. Black Broth, made of pork, blood, vinegar, salt and heavy seasoning was a main dish.

Apicius, a first-century Roman, wrote the earliest cookbook still in existence. His barley soup was made by boiling crushed barley with lentils, peas and chick peas. He mentions a purée of lettuce leaves and onions. There was also a liquid sweet-fruit dish of apricots cooked in honey, passum (dried grapes and must), wine and vinegar flavored with pepper, mint and a little liquamen (strained liquid from salted-down fish entrails, available commercially in trademarked pots as early as 400 B.C.). Apicius is said to have killed himself when his fortune ran out and he could no longer afford expensive, rare foods.

It was Athenaeus in 200 A.D. who wrote the most about food, seasonings and soup. His "Deipnosophists" (deipno - dining; sophist - sage) recounts endless dinner conversations which range over many subjects. Here are a few samples:

" 'No Lentils bring to me. They do taint the breath —no expensive dishes, but any of those vulgar lentils or what is called lentil soup.' And when everyone laughed, especially at the idea of lentil soup, he said, 'You are very ignorant men, you feasters, never having read any books of the Silli of Timon the Pyrrhonian. For he speaks of lentil soup as follows':

*"The Teian barley-cakes do please me not,*
*Nor e'en the Lydian sauces: but the Greeks,*
*And their dry lentil soup, delight me more*
*Than all that painful luxury of excess."*

## THE MIDDLE AGES TO MODERN SOUPS

In early times soup was called pottage (from pot and the latin *potare,* to drink). But during the Middle Ages the word "soup" (thought to be onomatopoeic of the sound of slurping hot liquid from a spoon) established itself in every European language, largely supplanting "pottage" except for "potage" in France. Some variations are: *Soop, sopa, sope, soepe, suppa, soppe, soep, suppe, soppa, sopero, soupe, chupe, zuppa, zup.* To "sup" was to eat the evening meal at which soup was traditionally served, and the meal itself became "supper."

In 1475, a Venetian by the name of Platina published "De Honesta Voluptate," a cookbook and guide to living with "honest indulgence and good health." With complete candor, he commented on the merits of various foods. For example, according to him, lentils generate black bile and cause leprosy, while turnips "soothe the throat and arouse the passion."

His soup recipes range from potages of livers, lungs and intestines to Verzusum, a sweet soup that "cools the liver and checks the bile." It required 30 egg yolks to make his saffron broth; white broth contained a pound of ground almonds, 20 egg whites and softened white bread. Soups were always to be kept far enough away from the coals so as not to absorb the smoke. Many of them called for verjuice (acid liquor from sour fruit juice) or must (unfermented wine). Even though he said hemp potage was difficult to digest and caused squeamishness, its elaborate recipe was included, as well as one for an eel torta, which was to be served to one's enemies because it was so bad.

In 1669, The CLOSET of the Eminent Learned Sir Kenelme Digbie Kt., was published in London, and contained the following soup recipes:

*"Barley Pôtage* — Take half a pound of French-barley, and wash it in three or four hot waters; then tye it up in a course linnen-cloth and strike it five or six blows against the table; for this will make it very tender . . . and let it mittoner a while upon the Chafing-dish, then serve it in."

*"Portugal Broth, as it was made for the Queen* — Make a very good broth with some lean of Veal, Beef and Mutton, and with a brawny Hen or young Cock. . . . . and when the broth is very good, you may drink it so, or, pour a little of it upon tosted sliced bread, and stew it, till the bread have drunk up all that broth, then add a little more, and stew; so adding by little and little, that the bread may imbibe it and swell: whereas if you drown it at once, the bread will not swell, and grow like gelly."

*"Potage de santé* of Mounsieur de S. — Put a knuckle of Veal and a Hen into an earthen Pipkin with a Gallon of water (about nine of the Clock forenoon) and boil it gently. When no more scum riseth (which will be in about a quarter of an hour,) take out the Hen (which else would be too much boiled,) and continue boiling gently till about half an hour past ten. Then put in the Hen again, and a handful of white Endive. Near half hour after eleven, put in two good handfuls of tender Sorrel, Borage, Bugloss, Lettice, Purslane a handful a piece, a little Cerfevil, and a little Beet-leaves. When he is in pretty good health, that he may venture upon more savoury hotter things, he puts in a large Onion stuck round with Cloves, and sometimes a little bundle of Thyme and other hot savoury herbs; which let boil a good half hour or better, and take them out, and throw them away. . . . .

"The Queen Mothers *Pressis Nourissant* was thus made. Take un Gigot of Mutton, a piece of

Veal, and a Capon (or half the quantity of each of these) and put them on to rost with convenient fire, till they are above half rosted, or rather, till they be two thirds rosted. Then take them off, and squeese out all their juyce in a press with screws, and scum all the fat from it, and put it between two dishes upon a Chafing-dish of Coals to boil a very little, or rather but to heat well; for by then it is through hot, the juyce will be ripened enough to drink, where-as before it was raw and bloody; then if you perceive any fat to remain and swim upon it, cleanse it away with a Feather. Sqeese the juyce of an Orange (through a holed spoon) into half a Porrenger full of this, and add a little Salt, and drink it. The Queen used this at nights in stead of a Supper; for when she took this, she did eat nothing else. It is of great, yet temperate nourishment. If you take a couple of Partridges in stead of a Capon, it will be of more nourishment, but hotter. Great Weaknesses and Consumptions have been recovered with long use of this, and strength and long life continued notably. It is good to take two or three spoonfuls of it in a good ordinary bouillon. I should like better the boiling the same things in a close flagon in bulliente Balneos as my Lady Kent, and My Mother used."

During the 18th century, references to soup occasionally appeared in English literature. In 1724, a manual on swift service advised, "Let the Cook daub the Back of his new Livery; or when he is going up with a Dish of Soup, let her follow him softly with a Ladle-full." Also, in the mid 1700's, the British Navy developed its famous "portable soup, a grey, dehydrated powder which will keep in canisters indefinitely."

By the 19th century, the word "soup" had become the source of some strange expressions. The term "soup-shop," according to the London Journal, referred to those establishments where burglars and thieves disposed of any silver or gold plate which fell into their hands. In such places, the melting pots were always kept ready. In Ireland, Protestant clergymen who sought converts by dispensing soup as charity were called "soupers." In 1890, the Catholic News commented, "Our readers are no doubt aware of the usual falsehoods employed by soupers for this purpose."

Meanwhile, 1890 Chicagoans were presumably poring over a newly published "Compendium of Cookery together with the Book of Knowledge, or 1000 ways of getting rich." Along with the Bible it apparently handled all of life's problems. It offers a "tonic for reformed drunkards to restore the vigor of the stomach." On the other hand it prescribes: "Fever and Ague — Four ounces galangal-root in a quart of gin, steeped in a warm place; take often."

More intriguing is its advice on how "To Restore From Stroke of Lightning — Shower with cold water for two hours; if the patient does not show signs of life, put salt in the water, and continue to shower an hour longer." What then? Its soups section sounds a little more practical:

• *Stock Soup* — .... basis of many of the soups ..... Time: Five and one-half hours. Average cost, twenty-five cents per quart.

• *White Stock Soup* — .... Strain off the liquor; rub the vegetables through the colander ..... and, as is your Saturday custom, put into a wide-mouth jar or a large bowl. ...

Potatoes, if boiled in the soup, are thought by some to render it unwholesome, from the opinion that the water in which potatoes have been cooked is almost a poison.

• *Mutton Soup* – Three pounds perfectly lean mutton. The scrag makes good soup and costs little. Two or three pounds of bones well pounded . . . . . Send around grated cheese with this soup.
• *Chicken Cream Soup* – Boil an old fowl, with an onion, in four quarts of cold water, until there remain but two quarts . . . .
• *Potato Soup* – Get as many beef or ham bones as you can, and smash them into fragments . . . .
• *Game Soup* – Two grouse or partridges, or if you have neither, use a pair of rabbits . . . . .
Simultaneously in San Francisco was published: "Scammell's Universal Treasure-House of Useful Knowledge, an Encyclopedia of Valuable Receipts in the Principal Arts of Life, including complete treatises on Practical chemistry; the prevention and cure of disease; household and culinary art; agriculture and stock-raising; the mechanical arts; mercantile life and laws; arts of refinement; recreations, etc." The soups include:
• *Calf's Head* – Parboil a calf's head; take off the skin and cut it into pieces of about 1-1/2" square; mince the fleshy part into smaller pieces; take out the back part of the eyes, and cut the remainder into rings; skin the tongue; cut it into slices; turn the whole into 3 qts of good stock . . . . .
• *Celery* – 9 heads of celery; 1 teaspoonful of salt, nutmeg to taste,; 1 lump of sugar; 1/2 pt. of strong stock; 1 pt. of cream; 2 qts. of boiling water; cut the celery into small pieces; throw it into the water . . . . . . .
• *Lentil* – Take 3/4 lb. of lentils; pick, wash and set on the fire with cold water, just enough to cover; do not cook in an earthen pot, as they will not get soft . . . . . . .

• *Consommé* – 6 lbs of lean beef; an old fowl, with the giblets, and any pieces of bone that you may have . . . . .
• *Curry* – Cut the meat from an ox cheek; soak it well . . . .
• *French* – Clean nicely a sheep's head . . . . . strain all off; cut the head into pieces and serve in the soup.
• *Herb* – Slice 3 large but young cucumbers; a handful of spring onions and six lettuces . . . . .
• *Mock Turtle* – Take 1/2 a calf's head . . . . procure a tin of mock turtle soup, boil this up with stock . . . The mixture of the stock made from fresh vegetables, with the preserved soup, will correct the slight taste of tin, which is the only objection which can be urged against it; and when a small quantity only of soup is required it will save time, trouble and expense to make it in this way, rather than to prepare it at home.
• *Mutton* – Take a shoulder of good heavy mutton weighing about 4 lbs; remove the skin and fat . . . . .
• *Pepper Pot* – Put 4 cow's feet and 4 lbs. of tripe to boil with water to cover them . . . . .

For years cookbook writers apparently felt responsibility for far more than food, and readers valued such books highly.
"The White House Cook Book, a comprehensive cyclopedia of information for the home containing cooking, toilet and household recipes, menus, dinner-giving, table etiquette, care of the sick, health suggestions, facts worth knowing, etc., New York, Akron, Chicago 1905 was dedicated 'To the wives of Our Presidents, those noble women who have graced the White House.' " One copy was inscribed by its owner, "This book belongs to Mrs. Nellie P. Doane, she wants it

and needs it and is a scratching, biting, kicking hairpuller. So beware."

Among the soup recipes are the following:

• *Plain Economical Soup* — Take a cold roast-beef bone etc., ... Serve this soup with sippits of toast. Sippits are bits of dry toast cut into a triangular form. A seasonable dish about the holidays.

• *Corn Soup* — Cut the corn from the cob, and boil the cobs in water for at least an hour, then add the grains . . . . .

• *Squirrel Soup* — Wash and quarter three or four good sized squirrels; put them on, with a small tablespoonful of salt, directly after breakfast in a gallon of cold water. Cover the pot close . . . . .

• *Mock Turtle Soup, of Calf's Head* — Scald a well-cleansed Calf's head, remove the brain, tie it up in a cloth, and boil an hour, or until the meat will easily slip from the bone . . . . .

• *Green Turtle Soup* — After removing the entrails, cut up the coarser parts of the turtle meat and bones. Add four quarts of water . . . . . At the end of four hours strain the soup, and add the inner parts of the turtle and the green fat . . . . . If there are eggs in the turtle, boil them in a separate vessel for four hours, and throw into the soup before taking up . . . . . . . Some cooks put in the green fat, cut into lumps an inch long. This makes a handsomer soup. Green turtle can now be purchased preserved in air-tight cans.

The Corona Club Cookbook, published in San Francisco in 1910 contains the following:

• *Wine Soup* — One quart boiling water, 1/2 teacupful of sago, the peeling of 1/2 a lemon; boil until sago is done, then add 1 teacupful of claret wine and sugar to taste.

• *Barley Water* — Teacup of pearl barley; add 2 quarts of water; boil in a double porcelain boiler 2-1/2 hours. Add 1 cup table raisins an hour before you remove it from the stove. It will look milky and a little thick. Squeeze the juice of 3 lemons in a pitcher, sweeten and salt it a little; strain the hot barley water over the above; pick out the raisins; put them in with the rest. Throw the barley away. To an invalid, it looks very inviting in a glass pitcher. Very acceptable to a fever patient.

• *Scraped Beef in Broth* — Buy 1/4 of a pound of round steak; be careful none of the dried edges of the meat are included in your purchase, as this sometimes poisons babies. Sear on hot griddle to retain the juice. Split in two and scrape with a dull knife so that only the pulp and none of the fibre is retained. Put in broth with rice.

According to Escoffier, soups were considered commonplace until this century. Only recently have they been perfected and firmly established as part of a fashionable meal. Our ancestors would be amazed and delighted, I think, if they were to taste all of the varied soups that follow.

# Between the Lines

One person, tasting a soup with the tip of his tongue and inhaling its aroma, may immediately smile or frown. Another person will wait until all of his tastebuds report, then will ponder a while before judging. Both may reverse their opinions after noting lingering aftertastes. Not only tasting methods, but also taste preferences vary widely. luckily, soups, unlike angelfood cake, can always be adjusted to suit particular tastes.

Certain distinct flavors like lemon, garlic, tomato, pepper and cumin can easily dominate a soup or offend ordinary palates if used to excess. Therefore, *soup* hews to a light touch. After all, a sorrel soup should taste like sorrel, an avocado like avocado, and no one wants a guest to say, "Ugh!" A light touch with servings is equally important. An overpowering portion can turn even the finest soup into a disaster. For a Maharajah offer more curry; for a Latin-American, more chili powder; for a gourmand, another serving.

Don't let prejudices hem you in. Distasteful seasonings can blend delightfully into unfamiliar surroundings. A new try at a food given up at age ten may be a pleasant surprise. Use each recipe as is before improvising.

• Some flavors blend; some complement and retain their identity; some merely clash or cancel each other. Certain seasonings don't come out without long steeping; others fade fast and must be added at the last minute.

• Cold soups flooding the tongue with soothing coolness slowly contact tastebuds which hot soups rarely reach, permitting appreciation of more delicate flavors. Hot soups tend to travel quickly along the top of the tongue for immediate swallowing and need stronger seasoning.

• Know the strength and flavor of each of your herbs and spices, particularly blended powders like curry and chili. Dried herbs should be used unless otherwise noted, but fresh are a delight and easily grown. Treble the measurements when using fresh.

• Fresh chives or Chinese (garlic) chives are worth growing outdoors or indoors in a pot.

• Many's the soup that has been changed from "very good" to "spectacular" with tasty, colorful garnishes.

• Don't be deterred by occasional unpleasant preparation odors; seafood and Oriental soups will purge themselves before serving. Let your exhaust fan help clear the air.

- Use freshly grated nutmeg, black pepper and cheese. If you prefer coarsely ground salt, grinder and bulk salt are available in specialty shops. Peppercorns release more flavor if crushed before using when recipes call for whole peppercorns.
- A bitter cucumber will ruin a soup. Taste first.
- If your blender won't purée smoothly, sieve afterwards when you want smooth texture.
- Tailor portions and select containers to fit the occasion—brunch, main lunch dish, cocktail stopper, dinner overture, midnight snack, etc.—and the weather.
- Vegetarians will find substituting vegetable stock and perhaps fortifying with vegetable stock base in any recipe gives a flavorful soup.
- Whether using whole, pressed or minced, smash garlic buds with the flat of a large knife or cleaver to remove skin easily and release more juices.
- Shallots are special and impart a unique flavor, so better not use a substitute.
- When thickening with egg yolk and cream liaison, always wait until the last minute; reheating or keeping warm will curdle the soup.
- Green pepper varies so widely in taste and strength it needs pretasting.
- Sorrel is not yet available in most markets, but is easily grown and does grow wild if you know where to find it. Although I have never used bottled or canned sorrel I understand it can be substituted.
- Try growing your own watercress or curlycress in a shady spot with lots of water. It reseeds itself and you always have a last-minute garnish. When larger quantities are needed, try to buy it in Oriental stores where quality is often better and bunches larger.
- Chervil, if seeds are fresh and sun is not too hot, grows as well as parsley. It's more feathery with a delicate licorice flavor that is quite different.
- Italian parsley is not as pretty as the curly variety for garnishing, but it has a stronger flavor and is just as easy to grow. Be sure to cut some stems when using parsley in cooking, as the flavor is stronger in the stems.
- See how gelatinous your stock is before making a cold soup. If it may make the soup too thick, thin with water and stock base before using.
- Bouquet garni: Tie given herbs in cheesecloth for easy removal from pot.
- Sour cream substitute may be used instead of dairy sour cream. It's consistency is a little firmer, so it should be beaten before using.
- Chinese parsley, cilantro and fresh coriander are the same. The taste is unique and not favored by all. The flavor varies with the age of the plant and as you become used to it you might change your mind if at first you didn't like it. Easily grown at home; seeds can be obtained in Oriental markets or hardware stores. It needs partial shade in hot areas; treat as chervil and use the stems as with parsley.
- All pasta products should be cooked *al dente!*
- Use the modern, light touch in cooking vegetables that are to retain their identity. Serve them tender-crisp, not mushy.
- Blanching is parboiling one to three minutes, then draining. When used to partially cook vegetables, a cold-water rinse stops cooking at the desired point. When blanching scum-prone ingredients like veal bones and turtle meat, rinse well after draining, then add to fresh cooking water in a clean pot.
- Good chicken stock base is hard to find, but is extremely useful for reducing gelatinous contents without diluting flavor, or for adding extra flavor when needed. San Fran brand, the only one I use, is top quality. Write P.O. Box 1074, San Rafael, California 94901.

# Stocks and Clear Soups

*Some foods are for lovers, some for philosophers,*
*some for tax collectors . . .*
*When one is near the grave, I prepare for him*
*some lentil soup, and make the crowning*
*meal of his life glorious.*

*—Athenaeus 200 B.C.*

## STOCKS AND CLEAR SOUPS

Simmer selected raw, precooked, or leftover morsels in water with butter or wine. Skim, strain out the leached solids, and season if desired. Cool, then refrigerate. Remove the solidified fat and you have the liquor or broth so vital to every soup chef—stock.

Sounds simple—until you consider the complexity of possible ingredients and flavors. While proportions are inexact, merely tossing anything and everything into a pot is not the answer. The ingredients must be good ones and they must be treated with care.

## BASIC STOCKS

Most commercially available concentrated stock bases are expensive, but they're good supplements to freshly prepared stocks.

*Leftovers:* Bones, scraps, carcasses, unserved portions, gravies, vegetable cooking water, vegetable tops, leaves and scrapings all are valuable in making stock as long as they're clean and kept refrigerated until added to the pot. Recycling in the kitchen is more than just an economy, it's a system of flavor saving, of cooking with your own array of delicious concentrates that are continually being modified, added to, and blended. Stocks are the flavor key not only to soups, but to many other gourmet dishes as well. For example, boiling fresh or frozen vegetables in stock instead of plain water.

*Cooking:* Cut up bones if possible. Start with cold water, cover, bring slowly to a rapid boil. Skim off any scum that rises to the surface. Turn down the heat and simmer, covered, 2 hours for leftover bones, 4 hours for fresh, adding vegetables and seasoning at the halfway point. Strain through coarse sieve into another kettle, then through a finer one into jars. Cool completely, put lids on jars, label, and refrigerate.

*Storing:* Fat acts as a sealer and solidifies under refrigeration, making it easy to remove. If stock is not used within ten days, it's best to return to the pot for a 2-minute boil, after which it can be refrigerated again. Stock can be frozen, but because freezing causes ingredients to separate it should be brought to a boil before using.

*Defatting:* If fresh stock is to be used immediately, skim off as much surface fat as possible, then float an ice cube to congeal the rest. A piece of chilled lettuce will collect fat on its surface.

*Clarifying:* To each quart of stock add 1 egg white beaten slightly with 2 teaspoons cold water and 1 crumbled egg shell. Stir and heat to boiling. Boil 2 minutes, remove from heat and let stand without stirring 20 minutes. Pour through strainer lined with double cheesecloth.

*Concentrating:* For richer, more flavorful stock, boil down strained stock to reduce water content.

# Stocks from Fresh Bones

## VEAL STOCK

2 pounds veal knuckle bone with meat, cut up
2 pounds veal shin bones, cut up
1 pair pig's feet (optional)
4 quarts water
2 carrots, chopped
2 onions, chopped
2 leeks and some tops, chopped
2 celery stalks and tops, chopped
2 turnips, chopped (optional)
2 garlic cloves (optional)
6 parsley sprigs
1 thyme sprig
1 bay leaf
2 teaspoons salt
6 peppercorns
1/2 teaspoon turmeric

*White Stock:*
Cover bones with 2 quarts of the water, bring to rapid boil, drain and rinse bones. Return to clean soup kettle and add 2 quarts water. Cover, bring slowly to rapid boil, skim off any more scum that may rise to top, cover, and simmer 2 hours.
Add remaining ingredients and simmer 2 more hours. Strain, jar, cool, cover and refrigerate.

*Brown Veal Stock:*
Brown bones in 3 tablespoons oil and/or butter. Simmer 2 hours, add browned vegetables and continue cooking 2 more hours.

## BEEF STOCK

4 pounds beef bones with meat, cut up
1 - 2 pounds marrow bones, sawed into 3-inch pieces
1 pair pig's feet (optional)
3 quarts cold water

3 carrots, chopped
2 celery stalks and tops, chopped
2 turnips, chopped
2 whole onions, each stuck with 2 cloves
1/2 cup diced tomatoes (optional)
1/4 cup diced green pepper (optional)
6 parsley sprigs
1 thyme sprig
1 oregano or marjoram sprig
1 bay leaf
2 cloves garlic (optional)
6 peppercorns
1 tablespoon salt

*Brown Stock:*
Put bones and pig's feet in large soup kettle and add water. Cover kettle, bring slowly to rapid boil, skim off any scum that may rise to top and simmer 2 hours.
Add rest of ingredients and continue cooking 2 more hours. Strain, jar, cool, cover and refrigerate.

*Dark Beef Stock:*
Brown bones in butter and/or oil in soup kettle or hot oven. Add browned vegetables after 2 hours.

## CHICKEN STOCK

6 pounds chicken backs, necks, and wing tips, cut up
3 quarts cold water

2 onions, chopped
2 carrots, chopped
1 turnip, chopped
2 celery stalks and tops, chopped
2 leeks and tops, chopped
2 garlic cloves
1 bay leaf
6 parsley sprigs
1 thyme sprig
1 savory sprig
1 tablespoon salt
1 teaspoon turmeric
1/2 teaspoon poultry seasoning

*White Stock:*
Put bones and water in soup kettle, cover and bring slowly to rapid boil. Skim off any scum that may rise to top and simmer 2 hours.
Add remaining ingredients and simmer 2 more hours. Strain, jar, cool, cover and refrigerate.

*Brown Chicken Stock:*
Brown bones in 3 tablespoons butter and/or rendered chicken fat in kettle or hot oven. Simmer 2 hours, add browned vegetables, and continue cooking 2 more hours.

## PORK STOCK

Follow directions for chicken stock, substituting pork bones for chicken bones, sage for turmeric; add 1 oregano sprig.

## LAMB STOCK

Follow directions for beef stock, substituting lamb blocks or other bones for the beef and adding 1 sprig rosemary.

## VEGETABLE STOCK

Use twice as much liquid as vegetables. Brown vegetables or not, as preferred, and use leftovers if desired. Tomatoes, lettuce, parsnips, leeks, turnips, broccoli stems, green pea pods, green beans, carrots, onions, asparagus ends, green onion tops, herbs and spices.

## FISH STOCK

2 cups each white wine and water
2 pounds fish heads, bones, shells
1 onion, chopped
3 parsley sprigs
1 bay leaf
1 thyme sprig
2 tablespoons lemon juice
1/2 teaspoon tarragon
1 teaspoon grated lemon peel
6 peppercorns
2 cloves
1/2 cup mushroom stems or 1 teaspoon
   powdered mushroom
1 teaspoon salt
1 tablespoon butter or oil

Combine ingredients in kettle, cover, bring to boil, skim off surface scum and simmer 1 hour.
Strain, jar, cool, cover and refrigerate.

# Stocks from Leftover Bones

## STOCK FROM ROAST BEEF

6 or 7 cracked ribs of leftover rib roast of beef and
  any scraps
2 onions, chopped
2 carrots, chopped
2 stalks celery and tops, chopped
2 leeks, chopped
2 garlic cloves (optional)
3 tablespoons oil and/or rendered beef fat
6 peppercorns
8 parsley sprigs
1 thyme sprig
1 marjoram sprig
1 bay leaf
1/2 tablespoon salt
1 teaspoon mushroom powder
2 quarts cold water

Brown onions, carrots, celery and leeks in oil and/
or fat. Add to soup kettle with rest of ingredients,
cover, bring slowly to rapid boil, skim off any scum
that rises to the top, cover and simmer 2 hours.
Strain, jar, cool, cover and refrigerate.

## LAMB STOCK

Follow directions for roast beef stock, using leftover leg of lamb bones and scraps instead of beef
bones; add 1 sprig rosemary and 1 sprig oregano.

## PORK STOCK

Follow directions for roast beef stock, using leftover pork bones and adding 1 teaspoon sage and 1
sprig oregano.

## POULTRY STOCK

1 turkey carcass, or 2 chicken or duck carcasses
  plus any leftover scraps and giblets
2 onions, chopped
2 carrots, chopped
2 leeks, chopped
2 turnips, chopped
1 garlic clove
6 parsley sprigs
1 thyme sprig
1 bay leaf
6 peppercorns
1/2 tablespoon salt
1/2 teaspoon each poultry seasoning and turmeric
3 quarts cold water

Put all ingredients in soup kettle, cover and bring
slowly to rapid boil. Skim off any scum that may
rise to top, cover and simmer 2 hours. Strain, jar,
cool, cover and refrigerate.

## GAME STOCK

4 pounds venison bones and scraps, or pheasant
   or partridge carcasses, or rabbit bones,
   plus scraps and giblets
   (add veal knuckle bone if needed to
   make 4 pounds)
2 onions, chopped
2 carrots, chopped
2 celery stalks, chopped
1/4 pound salt pork, diced and blanched
2 garlic cloves
1 teaspoon salt
6 parsley sprigs
1 thyme sprig
1 bay leaf
2 cloves
1 teaspoon basil
4 peppercorns
1/2 teaspoon juniper berries (optional)
3 quarts cold water

Put all ingredients in soup kettle. Cover, bring
slowly to rapid boil, skim off any scum that may
rise to top, cover and simmer 2 hours. Strain and
boil to reduce to 2 quarts or less, as desired.
Jar, cool and refrigerate. Remove fat and clarify
before using.

18

## BOUILLON

Follow recipe for dark beef stock, adding 1 pound cut-up beef and 1 meaty veal knuckle. Simmer 5 hours, strain, chill, defat and clarify. Add dry sherry and Worcestershire sauce to taste.

## BEEF CONSOMMÉ

Follow recipe for dark beef stock, adding 1 large meaty veal knuckle and 4 chicken backs. Strain, reduce to concentrate, chill, defat and clarify.

## PETITE MARMITE

Follow general rule for making stock, using 1-1/2 pounds rump beef, cubed, 1 meaty veal knuckle, cut up, 2 beef bones, cut up, 4 chicken backs, 2-1/2 quarts water, 1 tablespoon salt, 3 peppercorns, 4 parsley sprigs and 1 thyme sprig. Cook 1 hour, add 2 chopped carrots, 1 chopped turnip, 1 chopped leek and some green, 1 onion stuck with 2 cloves, and 1 cup chopped celery and leaves. Cook 2 hours, strain, chill, defat and clarify.

## JELLIED BOUILLON

Soften 2 tablespoons gelatin in 1/2 cup cold water. Bring 4 cups clarified beef stock to boil and add gelatin to dissolve. Season with 1 teaspoon Worcestershire sauce and 2 tablespoons lemon juice or dry white wine. Cool and chill until set. Break up with fork and serve with garnish of choice.

## JELLIED MADRILENE

Combine 6 cups rich chicken or veal stock with 2 cups tomato purée. Simmer 30 minutes and add 2 tablespoons gelatin softened in 1/4 cup each cold water and beet juice. Heat to dissolve gelatin, cool and chill until set.

## TURKEY BROTH WITH AVOCADO

6 cups rich turkey broth

2 avocados, diced, sliced or cut in rings
lemon juice

Heat broth to boiling and adjust seasonings to taste. Sprinkle avocados with lemon juice and just before serving add to hot broth. Garnish with minced parsley.
Serves 6.
You may lace with dry sherry.

## CONSOMMÉ PRINCESSE

6 cups chicken, veal, and/or beef stock

1/2 cup fresh green peas or asparagus tips
1/2 cup shredded cooked chicken

1/4 cup grated Parmesan cheese
minced chervil

Bring stock to boil and adjust seasonings to taste. Add peas or asparagus and cook until just tender-crisp. Reheat with chicken and sprinkle with cheese and minced chervil.
Serves 6

## STRACCIATELLA

6 cups rich beef broth or consommé

6 eggs, beaten
1-1/3 cups grated Parmesan or Romano cheese
1/2 teaspoon salt
1/4 teaspoon black pepper
1 tablespoon minced Italian parsley

minced chives

Bring broth or consommé to boil and adjust seasonings to taste.
Beat eggs, cheese, salt, pepper and parsley. Gradually pour into boiling soup, stirring with a fork to make ribbons of egg. Cook a few minutes to set eggs. Serve garnished with minced chives.
Serves 6
Or add cooked tripolini and garnish with tomato dice.

## CHICKEN BROTH WITH MUSHROOMS

6 cups chicken broth

1 cup diced cooked chicken
1/2 cup sliced mushrooms, sautéed in
  1 tablespoon butter
1/4 pound cooked thin noodles or cooked rice

minced chervil or watercress

Bring broth to boil and adjust seasonings to taste. Add chicken, mushroom, and noodles or rice. Reheat and season with lemon juice. Garnish with minced chervil or watercress.
Serves 6

## CELERY FUMET

6 cups chicken stock
1-1/2 cups chopped celery and some leaves
1/2 cup chopped white of leeks
2 large tomatoes, peeled and diced
3 tablespoons butter

minced celery leaves

Steam vegetables in butter, covered, 20 minutes. Add stock and cook 30 minutes.
Strain, adjust seasonings and garnish with minced celery leaves.
Serves 6

## CHICKEN BROTH WITH GIBLETS

6 cups chicken stock
1/2 teaspoon mushroom powder or
  1/4 cup chopped stems
1/2 cup each chopped onion, carrot, celery
  and leaves
1/4 cup diced core of cauliflower
2 shredded cabbage leaves
1 bay leaf
6 parsley sprigs

giblets from 2 or 3 chickens

minced parsley

Simmer stock, mushroom powder, vegetables, bay leaf and parsley 1 hour. Strain. Bring to boil.
Slice hearts and gizzards and add to boiling stock; cook 15 minutes.
Halve the livers, add to stock and cook 5 minutes. Sprinkle with minced parsley.
Serves 6

## GAME BROTH

6 cups clarified game stock
salt
pepper
thyme
12 chicken or game balls, cooked (see page 179)

minced chervil
Parmesan croutons

6 tablespoons dry red wine

Heat stock and adjust seasonings.
Add balls and garnish with minced chervil and Parmesan croutons.
Serve with a tablespoon of red wine in each bowl.
Serves 6

## TOMATO BOUILLON

4 cups chicken stock
1 14-ounce can Italian tomatoes

curry powder
lemon juice
pinch sugar

marrow dumplings (see page 177)

Cook stock and tomatoes 30 minutes. Force through food mill or sieve, reheat and season to taste.
Serve hot with marrow dumplings.
Serves 6
Or omit curry, lemon juice and dumplings. Add dry sherry or dry vermouth and serve icy cold.

## CLEAR OXTAIL BROTH

2-1/2 pounds oxtails, cut up
1/4 pound diced ham
1-1/2 cups chopped celery
1 cup chopped carrot
3/4 cup chopped onion
1/2 cup chopped turnip
1/4 cup chopped leek
3 tablespoons butter

6 cups water
2 savory sprigs
1 tarragon sprig
2 thyme sprigs
4 parsley sprigs
3 tablespoons catsup
1 cup port wine
1 teaspoon salt
1/2 teaspoon pepper

1-1/2 tablespoons butter
1 tablespoon flour

1 cup slivered meat from oxtails

minced parsley

Sauté oxtails, ham and vegetables in butter over high heat, stirring often, until golden.
Add water, herbs, catsup, port, salt and pepper. Cover, bring to boil and cook 3 hours until oxtails are tender. Skim surface scum whenever necessary. Strain, reserving oxtails. Cool, chill and defat.
Melt butter until bubbly, sprinkle with flour and cook and stir 3 minutes. Gradually add oxtail stock; cook and stir until smooth.
Adjust seasonings with salt, pepper, catsup and port. Reheat with meat and garnish with lots of minced parsley.
Serves 6

# VEGETABLE CONSOMMÉ

2 cups chopped onion
1 cup minced leeks
1/2 cup chopped celery root
1/2 cup chopped turnip and/or rutabaga
1 cup each chopped carrot and shredded cabbage
3 tablespoons butter

7 cups water
1 teaspoon salt
3 peppercorns
2 sprigs thyme
6 parsley sprigs
2 tablespoons fresh basil

minced fresh herbs

Sauté vegetables in butter, stirring, 10 minutes. Add water and seasonings, cover, bring to boil and simmer 2 hours.
Strain, adjust seasonings to taste and serve hot or cold with minced fresh herbs.
Serves 6

# DOUBLE MUSHROOM CONSOMMÉ

6 cups rich chicken, beef and/or veal stock

2 large dried mushrooms, soaked in water to cover
  with a pinch of sugar, until softened
3 green onions and tops, slivered
1/2 pound minced mushrooms

lemon juice
dry white wine
salt
pepper

raw mushrooms for garnish
lemon juice

Dice dried mushrooms and combine with stock, green onions and fresh mushrooms. Cover, bring to boil and simmer 45 minutes. Strain, pushing as much pulp through sieve as possible.
Season with lemon juice, wine, salt and pepper and serve with thinly sliced raw mushrooms rubbed with lemon juice.
Serves 6

## CONSOMMÉ PRINTANIER

6 cups rich consommé

3 tablespoons each julienned turnips and carrots,
  blanched and drained

1/2 cup cooked peas
1/2 cup cooked French beans, cut diagonally in
  small pieces

minced chervil
lemon slices

Bring consommé to boil, add turnips and carrots
and cook until almost done. Add peas and beans
and reheat. Vegetables should be tender-crisp.
Sprinkle with minced chervil and serve with lemon
slices.
Serves 6
May substitute asparagus tips and/or small kidney
beans for peas and beans.

## POACHED EGG CONSOMMÉ OR BROTH

6 cups rich consommé or broth

6 whole eggs

minced chives, parsley or chervil
toast or croutons

Bring stock to boil and adjust seasonings. Break an
egg into 6 heated bowls and pour hot soup over to
poach lightly. Garnish with finely minced chives,
parsley or chervil and serve with toast or croutons.
Eggs can be poached first if firmer eggs are desired.
Serves 6

## CONSOMMÉ BRUNOISE

6 cups rich stock

1/4 cup each finely shredded carrots, leeks
  and turnips
1/4 cup each thinly sliced celery and cauliflower
2 tablespoons butter

1/4 cup minced parsley

lemon peel

Sauté vegetables in butter until just tender-crisp.
Add to heated stock, stir in parsley and serve with a
garnish of tiny lemon peel.
Serves 6

## CELERY ROOT CONSOMMÉ

6 cups consommé

lemon juice
1 large celery root, peeled and sliced

minced parsley

Reserve 3 slices of celery root, cut them into
julienne and soak them in cold water and lemon
juice.
Cook consommé and remaining celery root slices
1 hour, strain and bring to boil. Add drained
julienne and cook until they are just tender-
crisp.
Sprinkle with minced parsley.
Serves 6

## SPAETZLE-SUPPE

6 cups stock of choice

*Spaetzle:*

1 beaten egg
1/2 cup milk
1 teaspoon melted butter
1/2 teaspoon salt
5 tablespoons flour

mixed fresh herbs

Combine eggs, milk, butter and salt. Beat in flour and force through a colander or spaetzle spoon into gently boiling stock. Cook 3 minutes until spaetzle rise to top. Simmer 3 more minutes.
Sprinkle with mixed fresh herbs.
Serves 6


## BROTH WITH MACARONI

6 cups rich broth
1/2 cup small shell macaroni
2 eggs, beaten with tiny bits of meat, liver, chicken
  or game and 1 teaspoon minced parsley

Bring broth to boil, add macaroni and cook until tender. Gradually drizzle egg mixture into gently boiling broth and cook until set.
Serves 6


## BEEF BROTH WITH DUMPLINGS

5 cups beef broth
1 cup dry red wine
1/2 teaspoon sugar
1/2 tablespoon lemon juice

1 recipe dumplings of choice

lemon slices

Heat broth, wine, sugar and lemon juice and adjust to taste.
Add cooked dumplings and serve with lemon slices.
Serves 6
Or omit wine and season 6 cups broth with tarragon and/or oregano. Garnish with tomato dice.


## CHICKEN-CLAM BROTH WITH ROYALES

5 cups rich chicken stock
1 cup clam juice

1 recipe royales  (see page 180)

6 teaspoons dry sherry

minced chives
paprika

Heat stock and clam juice; adjust seasonings to taste.


Divide royales between 6 heated bowls with a teaspoon of sherry in each. Ladle in hot broth and sprinkle with minced chives and paprika.
Serves 6
Or float a curl of spinach leaf in each bowl with a shred of carrot and a tiny lemon peel.

## PELMENY BROTH

6 cups rich stock

1 recipe pelmeny (see below)

minced chives
hot mustard
white vinegar
aji oil*

*see glossary

Bring stock to boil. Adjust seasoning. Place cooked pelmeny in bowls and ladle soup over it. Sprinkle with minced chives and pass hot mustard, white vinegar and aji oil.

## PELMENY

*Dough:*

1 scant cup flour
1/2 teaspoon salt
1/4 cup cold water
2 egg yolks

*Filling:*

1 pound ground beef or combination of beef,
  pork and veal
3 tablespoons grated onion
1/2 teaspoon salt
1/4 teaspoon black pepper
1/4 teaspoon powdered mushroom
1/2 teaspoon dill or Lemon Dill*

*see glossary

Mix dough ingredients and knead at least 10 minutes until smooth and elastic. Form into a ball and cover with inverted bowl for 1 hour. Roll into a rope 1/2-inch thick and cut off 1-inch pieces. Roll as thin as possible into 2-1/2-inch rounds.
Combine filling ingredients. Put 3/4 teaspoon filling on each round. Fold over to make half-moon shape and crimp edges to seal. Place on floured baking sheets and chill (or freeze) 30 minutes.
Cook in boiling salted water 7 minutes.

# Vegetable Soups

*"Beautiful soup! Who cares for fish*
*Game, or any other dish?*
*Who would not give all else for two*
*Pennyworth only of beautiful soup?"*
                    —Alice in Wonderland

The prosaic dried lentil, bean, and pea soups of the ancients lend themselves to a modern approach, for their bland flavors go well with a number of other ingredients. Potatoes, too, can be the basis of a whole family of soups. People usually think of vegetable soup as colorful green peas, diced carrots, onion rings, or other "fresh" vegetables in clear broth. All kinds of vegetable soups are included here.

The old-fashioned approach of soaking dried legumes overnight and then cooking them, and fresh vegetables, too, until completely soft (and usually mushy) is out of date as far as I am concerned. Vegetables should be cooked only enough to make them tender without destroying their crispness or leaching out their flavor, except, of course, when making stock or purées. Even most dried legumes, I think, should retain their shape and identity. Presoaking after washing and picking over need only consist of pouring boiling water over them and letting stand 2 hours, except in the case of chickpeas; longer soaking in water to cover allows them to swell and absorb liquid for shorter cooking later.

## FRESH ARTICHOKE SOUP

1 minced garlic clove
1/2 cup chopped onions
1 tablespoon olive oil
3-4 artichokes
3 cups beef or chicken stock
1 tablespoon lemon juice
1/2 tablespoon black pepper
1/2 tablespoon oregano

2 tablespoons chopped green onions, white
  part only
1 minced garlic clove
1 tablespoon butter

1 cup condensed cream of mushroom soup
1 cup half-and-half cream

1/2 teaspoon each salt and pepper
1/2 cup white wine

Sauté garlic and chopped onions in olive oil in a heavy kettle. Add artichokes, stock, lemon juice, pepper and oregano and simmer, covered, until artichokes are very tender, adding more water if needed. Remove artichokes, strain and reserve stock.

Scrape edible portion from the artichoke leaves, remove chokes and dice hearts, reserving one heart for garnish.

Sauté green onions and garlic in butter 3 minutes; purée in blender with artichokes and 1/2 cup of the reserved stock.

Blend soup and cream into purée; season with salt and pepper. Heat and adjust seasonings. Just before serving add wine and reserved diced artichoke heart.
Serves 4-6
Or add 1/4 cup tomato juice (or to taste) and reheat.

## CREAM OF BROCCOLI SOUP

2 - 2-1/2 pounds broccoli
1/2 cup chopped onion
1/4 cup minced green pepper
2 tablespoons butter and/or rendered chicken fat

2 tablespoons flour
6 cups rich chicken stock
bouquet garni of:
  1 bay leaf
  3 parsley sprigs
  1 thyme sprig
  6 peppercorns

1/4 teaspoon nutmeg or
  1/2 teaspoon curry powder
1/4 teaspoon white pepper

2 - 3 egg yolks
1 cup heavy cream
salt

slivered green onions
sour cream

Reserve 12 small broccoli flowerets and chop remainder. Sauté broccoli, onion and green pepper in butter and/or fat to brown slightly.

Sprinkle with flour, cook and stir 3 minutes and add stock and bouquet garni. Cook and stir until smooth and slightly thickened. Cover, bring to boil, and simmer 30 minutes until broccoli is soft. Discard bouquet garni.

Purée in blender and force through sieve to remove any stringy particles. Add nutmeg or curry and pepper.

Beat yolks and cream, whisk in 1/2 cup hot soup and return to rest of soup. Reheat; do not boil. Season with salt to taste and serve with slivered green onions and dollops of sour cream.

Serves 6 - 8

Or omit nutmeg or curry. Add 3 tablespoons tomato paste and mix well. Stir in 1 cup cooked macaroni, reheat and serve garnished with grated Parmesan cheese.

## BELL PEPPER

2 cups finely minced green pepper
1 cup minced onion
1/4 cup minced carrot
1 minced garlic clove
3 slices bacon, minced

2 cups canned tomatoes
4 cups beef and/or chicken stock
1/2 teaspoon salt
1/4 teaspoon black pepper
1/4 teaspoon basil
1 pound ground round steak

Sauté green pepper, onion, carrot, garlic and bacon until bacon is slightly browned.
Add tomatoes, stock, salt, pepper, basil and meat.
Cover, bring to boil, and simmer 45 minutes.
Adjust seasonings to taste.
Serve with garlic French bread.
Serves 6

# CREAMY CABBAGE SOUP

1/4 cup minced salt pork
2 tablespoons sweet butter
3 tablespoons minced shallots
1 minced garlic clove
1 tablespoon flour
5 cups chicken or beef stock
4 cups finely shredded Savoy cabbage
bouquet garni of:
   1 bay leaf
   2 parsley sprigs
   1 thyme sprig
   6 peppercorns
1 cup half-and-half cream or milk
3/4 cup sour cream
1/8 teaspoon nutmeg
1/4 teaspoon white pepper
1/2 teaspoon salt
2 egg yolks, beaten
1/2 cup heavy cream
minced parsley
grated Swiss cheese

Brown salt pork in butter, remove with slotted spoon and reserve.

Add shallots and garlic to pan and sauté until just golden.

Sprinkle with flour, cook and stir 3 minutes and gradually add stock. Cook and stir until smooth and slightly thickened.

Add cabbage and bouquet garni, cover, bring to boil and simmer 30 minutes. Discard bouquet garni and purée soup in blender.

Add cream or milk mixed with sour cream, reheat and season with nutmeg, pepper and salt.

Beat yolks with heavy cream, whisk in 1/2 cup hot soup and return to rest of soup. Reheat without boiling, and adjust seasonings with salt.

Garnish with reheated salt pork bits, minced parsley and grated Swiss cheese.

Serves 6 - 8

Or add tomatoes, or sautéed minced green pepper, and julienne of ham. Top with pimiento or sprinkle with caraway seeds.

## CREAM OF CELERY

2 cups celery and some tops, chopped
1 cup chopped onion
4 cups rich chicken stock

2 cups celery, thinly sliced on diagonal
1/2 cup chopped green leaves of celery
3 tablespoons each butter and flour

2 cups half-and-half cream
1/8 teaspoon nutmeg
1/4 teaspoon white pepper
1/2 teaspoon celery salt or Lemon Chef*

salt

chiffonade of sorrel (see page 180)

*see glossary

Simmer chopped celery and onion in stock 45 minutes. Strain.
Sauté sliced celery and leaves in butter 5 minutes, sprinkle with flour, cook and stir 3 minutes. Gradually add stock; cook and stir until smooth and slightly thickened.
Cover and simmer 15 minutes.
Add cream and seasonings and reheat.
Adjust seasonings with salt.
Just before serving add chiffonade of sorrel, a very important addition.
Serves 4 - 6
Or add 2 peeled, seeded and diced tomatoes when cooking thickened soup. Garnish with bacon bits or toasted almonds and minced parsley or top with grated cheese.

## CREAM OF CELERY ROOT

1-1/2 cups diced celery root
1/2 cup diced onion
2 tablespoons minced leeks
1 teaspoon minced garlic
3 tablespoons butter
1/2 teaspoon dry mustard
1/8 teaspoon sugar

2 cups chicken or veal stock

1 cup half-and-half cream

salt
white pepper
Lemon Celery*

3/4 cup tiny celery root julienne cooked in
   a little stock until tender
paprika
minced parsley

*see glossary

Sauté celery root, onion, leeks and garlic in butter 5 minutes. Sprinkle with mustard and sugar and cook and stir 5 more minutes.
Add stock, cover, bring to boil and simmer until celery root is tender. Purée in blender, add cream and heat without boiling. Season to taste with salt, pepper and Lemon Celery.
Serve garnished with celery root julienne and a sprinkling of paprika and minced parsley.
Serves 4
May also be served cold. Chill, adjust seasonings and serve in chilled bowls garnished with tiny lemon peel strips.

## CUCUMBER-CELERY MÉLANGE

1 cucumber, peeled, seeded and cut into
  1-inch julienne
2 ribs celery, thinly sliced on diagonal
1 leek, white only, minced
bouquet garni of:
  1 sprig thyme
  5 sprigs parsley
  1 bay leaf
  6 peppercorns

1-1/2 tablespoons flour
3-1/2 cups rich chicken stock
1/4 cup dry white wine

2 cucumbers, peeled, seeded and cut into
  1-inch julienne
1/2 teaspoon salt

1 egg yolk, beaten
1 cup heavy cream
1/2 teaspoon lemon juice
1/4 teaspoon each white pepper and
  Lemon Celery*

lemon slices
parsley sprigs

*see glossary

Steam cucumber, celery, leek and bouquet garni in butter, covered, until vegetables are soft.
Sprinkle with flour, cook and stir 3 minutes and gradually add stock and wine. Cook and stir until smooth and slightly thickened. Cover and simmer 10 minutes. Discard bouquet garni.
While soup is simmering, sprinkle cucumbers with salt and let stand in colander to drain. Rinse, drain and dry on paper toweling. Add to soup and cook 4 minutes.
Beat yolk and cream, whisk in 1/2 cup hot soup and return to rest of soup. Reheat but do not boil. Season and adjust to taste. Serve with lemon slices and tiny parsley sprigs.
Serves 4
Or add a chiffonade of sorrel (see page 180) in place of the lemon slices and serve with lemon croutons.

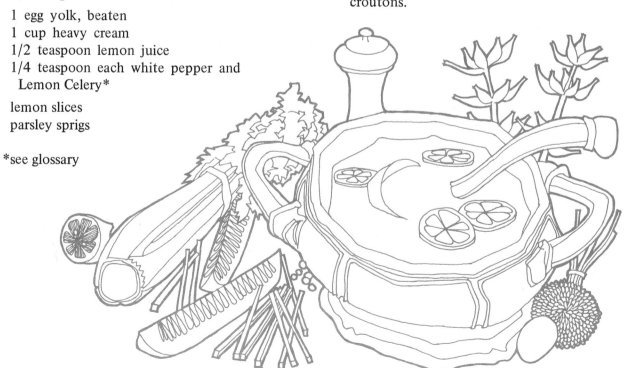

## GREEN SOUP

1/2 cup each finely chopped sorrel, spinach,
  dandelion greens, kale, Swiss chard or
  any green leafy vegetable or combination to
  make 2 - 3 cups
1/4 cup celery sliced thinly on diagonal
1/2 cup minced green onions and tops
1/4 cup minced leeks
1/4 cup minced parsley
1/4 cup minced watercress
3 tablespoons butter

1 tablespoon flour
4 cups rich game stock, or chicken stock or
  combination

1 cup sour cream

1/2 teaspoon salt
1/4 teaspoon black pepper
1 tablespoon lemon juice

paprika
toast fingers

Sauté vegetables, parsley and watercress in butter
until well coated and wilted.
Sprinkle with flour, cook and stir 3 minutes and
gradually add stock. Cook and stir until smooth.
Cover, bring to boil and simmer gently until celery
is just tender-crisp.
Remove from heat and beat in sour cream mixed
first with 1/2 cup of hot soup. Season and adjust to
taste. Sprinkle with paprika and serve with toast
fingers.
Serves 6
Or add little forcemeat balls of game (see page
179). Garnish with thinly sliced radishes.

## CARROT PURÉE

1-1/2 pounds carrots, sliced (4 cups)
1 stalk celery, chopped (1 cup)
3 cups chopped leeks with little green
1/2-inch piece bay leaf
6 parsley sprigs
6 cups rich chicken stock

1 cup heavy cream
3 tablespoons butter
1/8 teaspoon nutmeg
1/4 teaspoon white pepper
1/2 teaspoon Lemon Chef*

1/2 teaspoon brown sugar
1/4 cup heavy cream
1/2 cup grated carrot

salt
minced parsley or mint
croutons or toast rounds

*see glossary
Steam carrots, celery, leeks, bay leaf and parsley in
1 cup of stock until very soft. Remove bay leaf and
purée in blender, using more stock if needed. Force
through fine sieve, add rest of stock, cream, butter
and seasonings. Heat but do not boil.
Melt brown sugar in saucepan and cook and stir 3 -
4 minutes. Add carrots and cream, cover and cook
10 minutes until carrots are tender-crisp. Add to
hot soup, adjust seasonings, adding salt as needed,
and sprinkle with minced parsley or mint. Serve
with croutons or toast rounds.
Serves 6
Or sprinkle with grated onion, or float tiny balls of
Gorgonzola cheese rolled in paprika on top.

# EMMA'S MUSHROOM SOUP

1 pound round steak, cut into 1-inch cubes
1 teaspoon salt
4-1/2 cups water

1/2 cup butter
1/2 cup minced onions
1 pound fresh mushrooms, minced

2-1/2 tablespoons flour

1 cup half-and-half cream

salt

paprika
minced parsley

*For years Emma ruled the kitchen of a family who ate well, indeed. Now, years later her original recipe can still hold its own against those of famous chefs.*

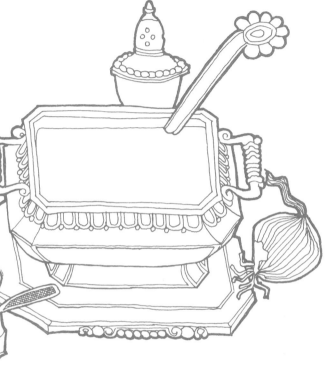

Sprinkle meat with salt, add cold water and let stand 1/2 hour. Cover, bring to slow boil, and simmer gently until meat is tender. Remove meat and reserve for another use or discard. Do not strain as the flavor of the "curds" that have formed enhances the soup.

Sauté onions in butter until soft but not brown. Add mushrooms, sauté and stir 5 minutes; sprinkle with flour, cook and stir 3 minutes, and gradually add broth. Cook and stir until slightly thickened.

Add cream and reheat; do not boil. Season with salt and serve sprinkled with paprika and minced parsley.

Serves 4 - 6

Or garnish with dollops of whipped cream.

33

## CREAMY ENDIVE SOUP

1-1/4 pounds French or Belgium endive
1/4 cup minced leeks
2 tablespoons minced shallots
3 tablespoons butter

1 cup diced potato
1 teaspoon chicken stock base
1/4 teaspoon Lemon Herb*
1/4 teaspoon white pepper
4 cups milk
2 cups half-and-half cream

salt
3 tablespoons butter bits

paprika
minced parsley
herb croutons

*see glossary

Sauté endive, leeks and shallots in butter 3 minutes, stirring to coat. Cover and cook over low heat 10 minutes.
Add potato, seasonings and milk; cover, bring to gentle boil and simmer 10 minutes or until potatoes are tender-crisp.
Add cream, reheat, adjust seasonings with salt, and swirl in butter bits.
Sprinkle with paprika and minced parsley and serve with herb croutons.
Serves 6 - 8

## CAULIFLOWER WITH CHEESE

4 cups cauliflowerets
4 cups chicken stock
1 teaspoon soy sauce
1/2 teaspoon each savory, paprika and
 garlic powder
1/4 teaspoon black pepper

2 tablespoons butter
2 tablespoons flour
1 cup evaporated milk

1/4 cup freshly grated Parmesan or Romano cheese

2 egg yolks, beaten
3 tablespoons lemon juice

Reserve 1/2 cup tiny flowerets for garnish. Cook remainder in stock with soy sauce, savory, paprika, garlic powder and pepper until cauliflower is soft. Purée in blender.
Melt butter until bubbly, add flour, and cook and stir 3 minutes. Gradually add milk; cook and stir until thickened and add purée and cheese. Reheat to melt cheese.
Beat eggs with lemon juice, whisk in 1/2 cup hot soup and return to rest of soup. Reheat; do not boil.
Garnish with reserved raw flowerets and extra cheese.
Serves 6

## SPINACH SOUP

1 pound fresh spinach, chopped (6 - 7 cups,
  loosely packed)
2 tablespoons minced green onions
1 minced garlic clove
3 tablespoons butter

1/8 teaspoon nutmeg
5 cups chicken, beef or veal stock

1 cup half-and-half cream
pinch sugar
1/2 teaspoon salt
1/4 teaspoon white pepper
1/4 teaspoon Lemon Chef*
butter bits

sieved hard-cooked eggs
paprika

*see glossary

Sauté spinach, green onions and garlic in butter,
stirring, until spinach is wilted.
Add nutmeg and stock, cover, bring to boil and
simmer 20 minutes. Purée in blender.
Add cream and seasonings, heat and adjust to taste.
Swirl in butter bits and sprinkle with sieved hard-
cooked eggs and paprika.
Serves 6
Or halve 3 small hard-cooked eggs, remove yolks
and mash them with 1-1/2 teaspoons softened
butter. Form balls and arrange in white halves,
garnish with a tiny parsley sprig, and float on hot
soup.

## CHERVIL SOUP

4 tablespoons butter
5 tablespoons flour
6 cups rich veal stock

1/2 cup minced chervil, firmly packed with
  only tender stems

2 - 3 egg yolks, beaten

1/4 teaspoon white pepper
1/2 teaspoon salt

minced chervil

Melt butter until bubbly, add flour, cook and stir
3 minutes. Do not brown. Gradually add stock,
cook and stir until smooth and slightly thickened.
Continue cooking, stirring occasionally, 30 minutes.
Add chervil, bring back to boil and cook 1 minute.
Beat yolks and 1/2 cup hot soup; return to rest of
soup and heat without boiling. Adjust seasonings to
taste with pepper and salt and serve with extra
minced chervil.
Serves 6
Or top with finely shredded iceberg lettuce.

# Potato Soups

## HOT POTATO SOUP

1-1/2 cups minced leeks, white and some of green
1/4 cup minced onion
1 large garlic clove, minced
3 tablespoons minced carrot
4 tablespoons butter and/or rendered chicken fat

4 cups chicken stock
1-1/2 cups diced potatoes

1/2 cup heavy cream

salt
white pepper
Beau Monde seasoning

Sauté leeks, onion, garlic and carrot in butter and/or fat until leeks are soft. Do not brown.
Add stock and potatoes, cover, bring to boil and simmer until potatoes are tender. Purée in blender. Add cream, reheat but do not boil, and season to taste with salt, pepper and Beau Monde. If too thick, thin with more stock or with half-and-half cream.
Serves 6
Or just before serving add 3 tablespoons dry vermouth or dry sherry. Or sprinkle with caraway seeds.

36

## CARROT-POTATO

1 recipe hot potato soup *without cream*

1 cup diced carrots
1/4 cup diced celery
3 tablespoons butter
1/2 teaspoon marjoram
pinch sugar

1/2 cup grated carrot

1 cup half-and-half cream

salt
pepper
marjoram

minced parsley

Sauté carrots and celery in butter until soft, sprinkling with marjoram and sugar as they are cooking. Purée in blender with some of the potato soup, combine with rest of soup, add grated carrots and simmer 5 minutes.
Reheat with cream and adjust seasonings to taste with salt, pepper and marjoram. Sprinkle with lots of minced parsley.
Serves 6
Or add 1/2 cup heavy cream, chill and garnish with raw grated carrots and minced parsley.

## CUCUMBER-POTATO

1 recipe hot potato soup *without cream*

1 large cucumber, peeled, seeded and grated
3 tablespoons grated onion

1 cup half-and-half cream

salt
white pepper
Lemon Celery or Lemon Dill*

minced fresh dill, slivered green onions or
  finely minced sweet pickle

*see glossary

Combine soup, cucumber and onion; simmer 10 minutes.
Reheat with cream. Do not boil.
Adjust seasonings to taste with salt, pepper and Lemon Celery or Lemon Dill.
Sprinkle with minced fresh dill, slivered green onions or finely minced sweet pickle.
Serves 6
Or add 1/2 cup heavy cream, chill and garnish with mint and sour cream.

## PEA-POTATO

1 recipe hot potato soup *without cream*

1 package frozen petite peas, thawed
1/4 cup minced celery
3 tablespoons butter

1 cup half-and-half cream

salt
white pepper
savory
butter bits
paprika

Sauté 1/2 package of peas and celery in butter until celery is soft.
Purée in blender with some of the soup; combine with rest of soup, rest of peas and the cream. Simmer 5 minutes.
Adjust seasonings with salt, pepper and savory, swirl in butter bits and sprinkle with paprika.
Serves 6
Or omit butter bits. Add 1/2 cup heavy cream, chill and serve with mint.

## BROCCOLI-POTATO

1 recipe hot potato soup *without cream*
1-1/2 cups cooked chopped broccoli
1-1/2 tablespoons grated onion
1 cup half-and-half cream

minced fresh dill or tiny, raw broccoli flowerets

Simmer potato soup, broccoli and onion 10 minutes to blend flavors. Purée in blender.
Reheat with cream and adjust seasonings to taste. Garnish with minced fresh dill or tiny raw broccoli flowerets.
Serves 6
Or add 1/2 cup heavy cream and chill. Serve with tiny shrimp.

## PARSLEY-POTATO

1 recipe hot potato soup *without cream*
1/4 cup diced celery
1 bunch parsley
3 tablespoons butter

1 cup half-and-half cream
1-1/2 cups minced parsley sprigs

salt
white pepper

lemon croutons

Remove stems from parsley and mince, reserving the sprigs. Sauté celery and stems in butter until celery is soft. Purée in blender with some of the potato soup, combine with rest of soup, cream and sprigs, and simmer 5 minutes.
Adjust seasonings to taste with salt and pepper. Serve with lemon croutons.
Serves 6
Or add 1/2 cup heavy cream, chill and serve with a sprinkle of paprika.

## WATERCRESS-POTATO

1 recipe hot potato soup *without cream*
1/4 cup diced celery
1 bunch watercress
3 tablespoons butter

1 cup half-and-half cream

salt
white pepper

garlic croutons

Sauté celery and the stems of the watercress minced, until celery is tender. Purée in blender with a little of the soup and combine with rest of soup, cream and the leaves of the watercress. Simmer 5 minutes, adjust seasonings with salt and pepper, and serve with lots of garlic croutons.
Serves 6
Or add 1/2 cup heavy cream, chill and serve with extra watercress.

38

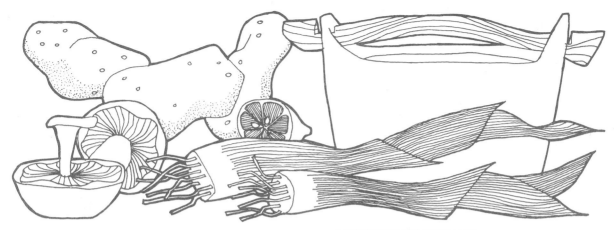

## SORREL-POTATO

1 recipe hot potato soup *without cream*

2 - 3 cups chopped sorrel
1 tablespoon butter and/or rendered chicken fat

1-1/2 cups half-and-half cream
2 egg yolks, beaten

salt
pepper
Lemon Herb*

paprika

*see glossary

Sauté sorrel in butter and/or fat 10 minutes, stirring occasionally.
Combine with soup and heat. Beat cream and egg yolks, whisk in 1/2 cup hot soup and return to rest of soup. Adjust seasonings to taste with salt, pepper and Lemon Herb.
Dust with paprika.
Serves 6
Or add 1/2 cup heavy cream, chill and garnish with chervil.

## MUSHROOM-POTATO

1 recipe hot potato soup *without cream*

1 cup finely minced mushrooms
1/4 cup each minced celery and green onions
3 tablespoons butter
1/4 teaspoon garlic powder
1/2 teaspoon lemon juice
dash oregano

1 cup half-and-half cream

salt
black pepper

paprika
minced dill or parsley

Sauté mushrooms, celery and green onions in butter until soft, sprinkling with seasonings as they cook. Purée in blender with some of the soup, combine with rest of soup, add cream and heat. Adjust seasonings to taste with salt and pepper.
Sprinkle with paprika and minced dill or parsley.
Serves 6
Or add 1/2 cup heavy cream, chill and garnish with dollops of sour cream and thinly sliced raw mushrooms that have been rubbed with lemon juice.

# Lentil Soups

Lentils, distinct in flavor, rich in protein and carbohydrates have thrived in the light dry soil of Mediterranean countries since at least 2200 B.C., providing soups and cereal for man, and fodder for animals. Magnifying lenses, when invented, were named after lentils because of their similar, rounded, convex surfaces. Peas and beans may be more popular as table food in the United States, but lentils will always retain their importance as an ingredient of soup.

## LENTIL SOUP

1 carrot, diced
1 onion, diced
1 rib celery, chopped
1 28-ounce can tomatoes
1 cup lentils
6 cups water
1 large ham hock

salt
pepper

Purée carrot, onion and celery in blender with a little juice from tomatoes.
Combine with tomatoes, lentils, water and ham hock; cover, bring to boil and simmer 3 hours. Remove ham hock; cut meat into strips. Add to soup, reheat and adjust seasonings with salt and pepper.
Serves 6

## BROWN LENTIL AND POTATO

4 slices lean bacon, minced
1/2 cup each diced carrots and onions
3/4 cup diced celery
1 minced garlic clove
2 tablespoons diced green pepper

1 cup lentils

2 cups water
3 cups beef or lamb stock
1/4 cup tomato paste
bouquet garni of:
  3 cloves
  1 bay leaf
  3 parsley sprigs
  1 thyme sprig
1/2 teaspoon salt
1/4 teaspoon black pepper

1-1/2 cups diced potato

1-1/2 tablespoons red-wine vinegar
salt and pepper
slivered green onions

Sauté bacon, carrots, onion, celery, garlic and green pepper until golden.
Combine with lentils, water, stock, tomato paste, bouquet garni, salt and pepper. Cover, bring to boil and simmer 1-1/2 hours.
Add potatoes, bring back to boil and cook 15 minutes. Remove bouquet garni.
Season with vinegar and adjust with salt and pepper. Sprinkle with lots of slivered green onions.
Serves 6 - 8
Or add cooked spinach and cooked sliced Italian sausages. Season with allspice.

## BROWN LENTIL WITH SAUSAGE

1/2 pound lentils
4 cups water
1/4 pound diced salt pork
1/2 cup each diced carrot, onion and celery
bouquet garni of:
  1/2 orange
  3 parsley sprigs
  1 bay leaf
  1 sprig thyme
1/2 teaspoon salt
1/2 teaspoon black pepper
2 tablespoons butter
1-1/2 tablespoons rice flour

beef stock (optional)
sour cream
2 cups sliced cooked garlic sausages
dry sherry

Combine lentils, water, salt pork, vegetables, bouquet garni, salt and pepper. Cover, bring to boil and simmer 1-1/2 hours or until lentils are tender. Discard bouquet garni.
Melt butter until bubbly, sprinkle with flour, and cook and stir 3 minutes. Gradually add soup; cook and stir until slightly thickened.
Thin with beef stock if thinner soup is desired.
Serve each portion with 1/2 tablespoon dry sherry, 1 teaspoon sour cream and sliced sausage.
Serves 4 - 6
Or sprinkle with paprika and minced parsley.

## LENTIL SOUP WITH FRESH PINEAPPLE

1 cup lentils
4 cups beef stock
3 tablespoons grated onion
3 pressed garlic cloves

2 large slices *fresh* pineapple, cut up

1 can consommé

sour cream

*This is not a pretty soup, but the combination of flavors is unusual and surprisingly good.*

Combine lentils, stock, onion and garlic. Cover, bring to boil and simmer 1 - 1-1/2 hours until lentils are almost tender.
Add pineapple and cook 10 minutes.
Add consommé, heat and serve with dollops of sour cream.
Serves 4 - 6

## MASUR LENTIL WITH WINE

1 cup red lentils

1/4 cup minced bacon or salt pork
1/2 cup minced onion
1/4 cup chopped carrot
1/3 cup chopped celery
2 tablespoons chopped parsley
1 minced garlic clove
1/4 teaspoon each oregano and savory
1/2 teaspoon salt
1/4 teaspoon pepper

2 cups beef stock
1 10-1/2-ounce can consommé
3/4 cup tomato juice
1 - 2 tablespoons lemon juice

2 tablespoons dry red wine

lemon slices
minced chives

Sauté bacon or pork, vegetables, herbs and seasonings until bacon or salt pork is browned.
Add lentils, stock and consommé, cover, bring to boil and simmer until lentils are soft.
Purée in blender, reheat with tomato juice and add lemon juice. Adjust seasonings to taste.
Just before serving add wine and serve garnished with lemon slices and minced chives.
Serves 4 - 6
Or add 1/2 cup finely chopped cooked spinach and sliced hard-cooked eggs.

## GARBANZO

# Bean Soups

2 cups chickpeas, soaked in 3 cups water overnight

1 cup minced onion
1/2 cup minced leeks
1/4 cup minced green pepper
2 teaspoons minced garlic
1/4 cup olive oil

4 cups rich beef or lamb stock
1 small ham hock
1 teaspoon paprika
1/2 teaspoon salt
1/4 teaspoon pepper
1/8 teaspoon saffron

2 garlic sausages, sliced and sautéed in
1/2 tablespoon butter

garlic croutons

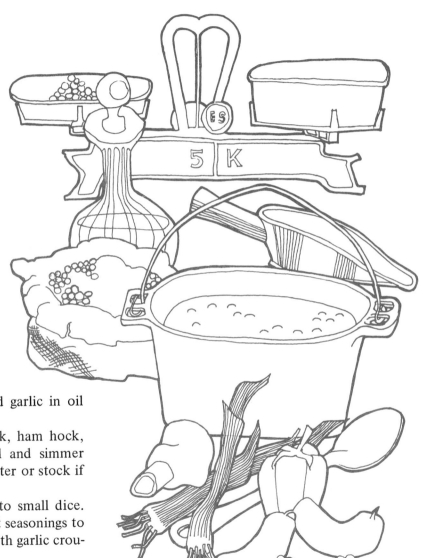

Sauté onion, leeks, green pepper and garlic in oil until onion is soft.

Add chickpeas and their liquid, stock, ham hock, and seasonings. Cover, bring to boil and simmer until chickpeas are tender, adding water or stock if needed.

Remove ham hock and cut meat into small dice. Return diced ham to soup and adjust seasonings to taste. Add sausage slices and serve with garlic croutons.

Serves 6 - 8

Or add diced potatoes the last 15 minutes of cooking and garnish with minced mint.

## WHITE BEAN

2 cups white beans
6 cups chicken stock
1 small ham hock
1 calf's tongue, blanched and rinsed
1 cup minced onions
1 cup chopped celery with some leaves
1/2 cup minced leeks
3 tablespoons butter
bouquet garni of:
  3 parsley sprigs
  1 thyme sprig
  1 bay leaf
  6 peppercorns
1/2 teaspoon salt
1/4 teaspoon white pepper
dash cayenne

4 tablespoons butter bits
1/2 cup minced parsley

paprika
horseradish

Sauté onions, celery and leeks in butter until onions are soft. Combine with beans, stock, ham hock, tongue, bouquet garni, salt, pepper and cayenne. Cover, bring to boil and simmer 2 hours.
Discard bouquet garni. Remove ham hock and tongue and cut as much into dice as desired. Return diced meat to soup, heat and adjust seasonings to taste.
Stir in butter bits and parsley and sprinkle with paprika. Pass horseradish and rye bread.
Serves 6 - 8
Or add 1 cup tomato juice and sliced Polish or garlic sausages, cooked.

## PINTO BEAN

1-1/4 cups pinto beans
1 ham hock
6 cups pork stock
1 cup chopped onion
1/2 cup chopped celery
1/4 cup each chopped leeks and carrot
1 minced garlic clove
3 tablespoons olive oil

1 28-ounce can tomatoes
bouquet garni of:
  2 cloves
  1 bay leaf
  6 peppercorns
  4 parsley sprigs
1 teaspoon salt
1/2 teaspoon black pepper

1 8-ounce can tomato sauce

minced cilantro

Sauté onion, celery, leek, carrot and garlic in oil until onion is soft. Add beans, ham hock, stock, tomatoes, bouquet garni, salt and pepper. Cover, bring to boil and simmer 3 hours. Discard bouquet garni.
Remove ham hock, cut meat into strips and reserve. Purée 2 cups of soup (with some beans) and return to rest of soup.
Add ham strips and tomato sauce, reheat and adjust seasonings.
Sprinkle with minced cilantro.
Serves 6 - 8
Or add 1 cup cooked spaghetti or other pasta.

## CREAMY WHITE BEAN

3/4 cup small white beans
1-1/2 cups water
1/2 teaspoon salt

1-1/2 cups thinly sliced onion
1/2 cup each chopped celery and
 celery leaves
1/2 cup chopped carrot
1/2 cup minced parsley
2 tablespoons each olive oil and butter

5 cups veal and/or chicken stock
1/2 cup tomato paste
1/2 teaspoon each basil and white pepper

1 cup half-and-half cream
salt

chiffonade of sorrel and spinach (see page 180)

Cook beans in salted water 1 hour, adding more water if needed.
Sauté vegetables and parsley in oil and butter, covered, 30 minutes. Do not brown.
Add stock, tomato paste, basil, pepper and beans with their liquid. Cover, bring to boil and simmer 1 hour or until beans are tender.
Purée in blender, reheat with cream and adjust seasonings to taste.
Serve with a chiffonade in each bowl.
Serves 6
Or ladle soup into 6 ovenproof bowls; sprinkle each with 2 tablespoons grated sharp Cheddar cheese and broil to melt cheese.

## CUBAN BLACK BEAN

1 pound black beans
8 cups water
2 tablespoons salt

1 cup minced onion
1 cup minced green pepper
3/4 cup minced celery
3/4 cup minced carrots
6 tablespoons olive oil

5 minced garlic cloves
1/2 tablespoon cumin
1 tablespoon white vinegar
1 teaspoon Maggi's seasoning

salt
pepper

minced raw onions
sieved hard-cooked egg yolk

*Highly seasoned soup that can be served as a main meal with rice.*

Simmer beans in salted water until soft.
Sauté onion, pepper, celery and carrots in oil until onions are brown. Add garlic, cumin, vinegar and Maggi's seasoning. Cook and stir 3 minutes.
Drain a little water from the beans, add to vegetables, and cook slowly, covered, 30 minutes. Combine with beans, adding more water if needed. Reheat and adjust seasonings with salt and pepper. Pass bowls of minced raw onions (soaked in olive oil and vinegar if desired) and sieved hard-cooked egg yolk.
Serves 8 - 10

# Romanic Soups

*Of soup and love the first is the best.*
*—Spanish Proverb*

Perhaps the Roman Empire left more than its language as a heritage to France, Spain, Italy and Portugal. These Mediterranean countries are all unsurpassed in the culinary arts, especially in imaginative soup making.

## FRENCH ONION SOUP GRATINÉE

4 cups thinly sliced onions
1/2 teaspoon sugar
1/4 cup butter and/or rendered chicken fat
1 tablespoon olive oil
1 finely minced garlic clove
2 tablespoons flour
1/4 teaspoon dry mustard
1/4 cup heated cognac
2 cups each beef and chicken stock
1 10-1/2-ounce can consommé
1/4 teaspoon nutmeg
1/8 teaspoon black pepper
1/2 teaspoon Worcestershire sauce

1/2 cup dry vermouth or dry white wine

6 rusks or sour dough French bread slices, toasted
6 tablespoons each grated Gruyère and
    Parmesan, or crumbled Gorgonzola, or
    grated Comte or Beaufort cheese

Slowly brown onions and sugar in butter and/or fat and oil. Add garlic, cook 3 minutes and sprinkle with flour and mustard. Cook and stir 3 minutes, raise heat and pour cognac over. Ignite and let burn down. Add stocks, consommé, nutmeg, pepper and Worcestershire sauce. Cover, bring to boil and simmer 20 minutes.
Cool and refrigerate overnight to mellow the flavor. Reheat and adjust seasonings to taste. Just before serving add vermouth or wine.
Ladle soup into ovenproof bowls, top with rusks or toast sprinkled with cheese and broil to melt cheese.
Serves 6
Or omit vermouth or white wine and season with dry red wine. Sprinkle with parsley and paprika.

## SOUPE DE COMPIÈGNE

1-1/2 cups diced onions
1/8 teaspoon sugar
4 tablespoons butter
1/2 teaspoon dry mustard
2 cups lamb stock

1 cup milk
1 egg yolk, beaten
1/2 cup heavy cream

salt
cayenne

slivered pimiento
minced parsley and/or chives

Sauté onions sprinkled with sugar in butter until starting to turn golden. Sprinkle with mustard and cook 2 minutes. Add stock, cover, bring to boil and simmer until onions are soft.
Purée in blender, add milk and heat. Beat egg yolk and cream, whisk in 1/2 cup of hot soup and reheat. Do not boil.
Adjust seasonings to taste with salt and cayenne and serve with a garnish of slivered pimiento and minced parsley and/or chives.
Serves 4
Or add a chiffonade (see page 180) of chicory and sprinkle with paprika.

## POTAGE FINES HERBES

1 cup chopped sorrel
1/2 cup each chopped lettuce, chervil and
  watercress
3/4 cup chopped leek
2 minced garlic cloves
2 teaspoons minced fresh dill
1 tablespoon butter

1/2 tablespoon flour

2 cups chicken stock
1 teaspoon chicken stock base
1 teaspoon minced fresh savory
1/2 teaspoon minced fresh basil
1 cup diced potato

1-1/2 cups half-and-half cream

2 egg yolks, beaten
1/2 cup heavy cream

watercress sprigs

Sauté herbs and vegetables in butter 5 minutes, stirring to coat well.
Sprinkle with flour, cook and stir 3 minutes and gradually add stock. Cook and stir until smooth.
Add stock base, savory, basil and potato. Cover, bring to boil and cook until potatoes are soft. Purée in blender.
Reheat with half-and-half.
Beat yolks and heavy cream, whisk in 1/2 cup hot soup and return to rest of soup. Heat, but do not boil. Adjust seasonings to taste.
Serve with sprigs of watercress.
Serves 4
Pass a jardinière of raw tomatoes, cooked peas, carrots, asparagus and/or beans.

## AUBERGINE PURÉE

1 (unpeeled) medium eggplant, diced (2-1/2 -
  3 cups),
1/4 cup minced mushrooms
2 tablespoons minced green onions and tops
1 minced garlic clove
2 tablespoons olive oil

3 cups lamb stock
pinch sugar
1-1/2 teaspoons tomato paste
1/4 cup dry red wine

1 tablespoon butter
1 tablespoon flour
1/4 teaspoon sage

3/4 cup heavy cream
salt
pepper

tomato dice
yoghurt

Sauté eggplant, mushrooms, green onions and garlic in oil, covered, 10 minutes. Stir frequently.
Add stock, sugar, tomato paste and wine. Cover, bring to boil and simmer until eggplant is soft.
Force through sieve and push as much pulp through as possible, leaving the skin.
Melt butter until bubbly, sprinkle with flour and sage, cook and stir 3 minutes. Gradually add eggplant stock; cook and stir until smooth and slightly thickened.
Add cream, reheat without boiling and adjust seasonings to taste with more sage, salt and pepper.
Garnish with tomato dice and pass a bowl of yoghurt.
Serves 4 - 6

## SOUPE DE LAITUE

3 cups shredded iceberg or romaine lettuce
4 cups rich beef stock
1 cup chopped watercress

3 tablespoons butter
1/4 cup minced onion
2 tablespoons green pepper
1 garlic clove, minced
1 teaspoon minced fresh tarragon, or
  1/4 teaspoon dried
2 tablespoons minced parsley
1/8 teaspoon nutmeg
1/8 teaspoon white pepper
2 tablespoons rice (optional)
1 cup half-and-half cream

2 egg yolks, beaten
3/4 cup heavy cream

salt

pepper

herb croutons

In blender chop lettuce a cup or so at a time, using stock if needed for moisture. Add to rest of stock with watercress.

Sauté onion, green pepper, garlic and herbs in butter until soft; add seasonings and combine with stock mixture. Add rice if desired. Cover, bring to boil, and simmer gently 30 minutes.

Add half-and-half cream and heat. Beat yolks into heavy cream, whisk in 1/2 cup hot soup, beat, and return to rest of soup. Reheat. Do not boil. Adjust seasonings to taste.

Serve with generous portions of herb croutons.

Serves 6

Or add cooked peas, chopped water chestnuts (canned) and minced green onions. Sprinkle with a bit of shredded raw lettuce.

# MUSHROOM VELOUTÉ

1 pound mushrooms, sliced (save 8 caps, slice and
  sauté in 1 tablespoon butter)
1/2 cup minced onion
1/4 cup minced celery
1 garlic clove, minced
3 tablespoons butter and/or olive oil
1/8 teaspoon dry mustard
1/16 teaspoon cayenne pepper
1/2 teaspoon Lemon Celery*
2 tablespoons flour
6 cups chicken or beef stock
3 parsley sprigs
1 thyme sprig or 1/2 teaspoon dried thyme

2 egg yolks, beaten
3/4 cup heavy cream
2 tablespoons butter, softened

salt

paprika
minced chervil

*see glossary

Sauté onions, celery and garlic in butter and/or oil
until soft; add mushrooms and seasonings and cook
until slightly browned. Sprinkle with flour, cook
and stir 3 minutes, and gradually add stock. Cook
and stir until smooth and slightly thickened.

Add parsley and thyme, cover and simmer 30 minutes. Strain.

Add reserved caps, simmer 5 minutes; beat yolks
with cream; whisk in 1/2 cup hot soup and return
to rest of soup. Reheat but do not boil. Swirl in
butter, adjust seasonings and serve with sprinkle of
paprika and minced chervil.

Serves 6

Or omit the liaison of yolks and cream, add 1/3 cup
dry sherry and 1/2 cup half-and-half. Pour into
ovenproof bowls, spread with salted whipped cream
and slivered almonds, and broil briefly to brown
cream.

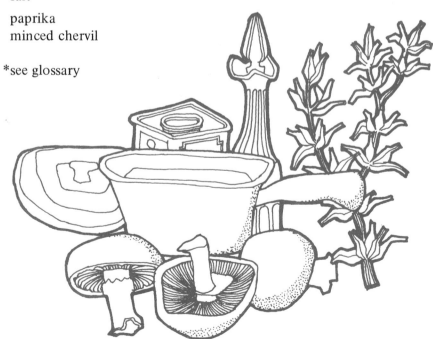

## POTAGE PAYSANNE

4 cups chicken stock
1 tablespoon beef stock base
1/2 cup minced leek with some green
1 chopped carrot
1 chopped turnip
1 diced potato
1/2 package 10-1/2-ounce frozen peas
4 cabbage leaves
6 lettuce leaves
6 sprigs each parsley and watercress

6 - 8 large fresh mint leaves
1 tablespoon fresh dill

1 cup half-and-half cream
2 tablespoons lemon juice
2 tablespoons butter
1/4 teaspoon black pepper
1/2 teaspoon salt

sour cream

Simmer stock, stock base, vegetables, parsley and watercress until vegetables are soft.
Add mint and dill; purée in blender.
Reheat with cream, lemon juice and butter. Season with pepper and salt and adjust to taste.
Serve with dollops of sour cream.
Serves 6
Or garnish with chopped watercress and tomato dice. For heartier soup add cooked sliced sausage. Dry vermouth adds a special zest.

## POTAGE DUBARRY

4 cups cauliflowerets
1 cup each chopped celery and onion
1/4 cup chopped carrot
3 tablespoons butter and/or rendered chicken fat

2 tablespoons rice flour

3 cups chicken or veal stock

1/4 teaspoon each garlic powder and pepper
dash cayenne

1 cup milk
1 cup half-and-half cream

1 teaspoon curry powder
2 teaspoons lemon juice
salt

minced parsley

Reserve 1/2 cup tiny flowerets for garnish. Sauté remainder with celery, onion and carrot in butter and/or fat until well coated and softened.
Sprinkle with flour, cook and stir 3 minutes and gradually add stock. Cook and stir until smooth and slightly thickened.
Season with garlic powder, pepper and cayenne, cover and simmer 30 minutes. Purée in blender, add milk and cream, and heat.
Add curry, lemon juice and salt and adjust to taste.
Garnish with reserved raw cauliflowerets and minced parsley.
Serves 6

## POTAGE GERMINY

4 cups chopped sorrel
2 tablespoons butter
2 tablespoons rendered chicken fat

1 tablespoon flour
4 cups rich chicken stock
1/4 teaspoon white pepper

3 egg yolks, beaten
2 cups half-and-half cream

salt
lemon juice or dry sherry or Madeira

paprika
minced parsley

Sauté sorrel in butter and fat until limp and discolored.

Sprinkle with flour, stir and cook 3 minutes, and gradually add stock. Cook and stir until smooth and slightly thickened. Season with pepper, cover, bring to boil and simmer 15 - 20 minutes, stirring occasionally. Purée in blender.

Beat egg yolks and cream, whisk in 1/2 cup hot soup and return to rest of soup. Reheat without boiling.

Adjust seasonings to taste with salt and lemon juice. Or season with sherry or Madeira. Sprinkle with paprika and minced parsley and serve with lemon toast fingers.

Serves 6

Basil, marjoram and lovage compliment sorrel; if you have an herb garden use them.

## SORREL BROTH

2 cups minced sorrel, firmly packed
6 cups rich chicken broth

3 eggs, beaten

1/4 cup dry sherry
minced parsley
herb croutons

Simmer sorrel and broth 15 minutes.

Whisk 1/2 cup hot broth into beaten eggs and return to rest of soup. Reheat without boiling.

Adjust seasonings to taste, add sherry, sprinkle with minced parsley and serve with herb croutons.

Serves 6

Or add finely shredded lettuce and minced chervil to the sorrel.

## POTAGE SAINT-CLOUD

6 cups fresh shelled peas
6 cups chicken stock
bouquet garni of:
  1/2 onion
  1 garlic clove
  1 sprig thyme
  1 sprig chervil
  4 sprigs parsley
  1/2 teaspoon basil
  2 green onions and tops, cut up
  1 bay leaf
1 teaspoon turmeric

1/2 teaspoon salt
1/4 teaspoon pepper
1 teaspoon curry powder
3 tablespoons butter bits

reserved peas
minced chervil

Combine peas, stock, bouquet garni and turmeric; cover, bring to boil and cook 5 minutes until peas are just tender-crisp. Remove 1/2 cup of peas and reserve. Continue cooking remaining peas 30 minutes. Purée in blender.

Season with salt, pepper and curry and adjust to taste. Swirl in butter bits.

Serve with reserved peas and a sprinkle of minced chervil.

Serves 6

Or omit butter bits and curry. Add 1 cup heavy cream and season to taste with dry sherry. Garnish with crab legs.

## AMBASSADEURS

Use lamb stock, add a chiffonade (see page 180) of sorrel and 1 cup cooked rice, and serve hot.

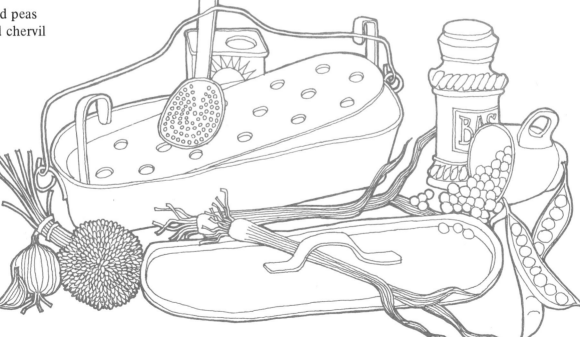

# Spanish Soups

According to Jorge Rosell and his wife, former Catalonians who now operate a fascinating grocery import store in San Francisco, gazpacho is served with green tomatoes and is more a salad than a soup. They offer the following six soup ideas as truly representative of Catalonia, Spain, where garlic, onion, and pimentón in descending order are the most popular seasonings.

SPANISH PUMPKIN SOUP

6 cups chicken or beef stock
2 pounds fresh pumpkin*, peeled and cubed
4 minced garlic cloves
1-1/2 cups minced onion
1/4 - 1/2 cup minced cilantro

salt
black pepper
bread cubes fried in garlic olive oil
cilantro sprigs

*Imported from Puerto Rico almost any time of the year and available in Mexican markets. Lighter, more delicate flavor than ours.

Combine ingredients and cook until pumpkin is tender. Purée in blender, reheat and adjust seasonings with salt and pepper.
Serve hot with bread cubes fried in garlic olive oil, and garnish with extra cilantro.
Serves 6 - 8
Flavor of cilantro grows stronger if soup is made ahead and reheated. Can be served cold if nongelatinous stock is used.

## SOPA DE JUDIAS BLANCOS

1 cup white beans, rinsed and drained
6 cups water
4 garlic cloves
1 quartered onion
1 ham hock
1/2 teaspoon salt

1 wedge cabbage (1/8 head)
1 whole carrot, halved
1 small rib celery, halved

garlic croutons

Tie garlic, onion and ham hock in cheesecloth for easy removal.
Combine with beans, water and salt. Cover, bring to boil and simmer 1-1/2 hours or until beans are almost tender.
Tie cabbage, carrot and celery in cheesecloth and add to soup; continue cooking until vegetables are tender, adding water as needed.
Remove vegetables and ham hock; serve with garlic croutons.
Serves 4 - 6
Or add tomatoes if desired. Serve ham, cabbage, carrot and celery on side for heartier meal.

## SOPA DE GALLINA

6 cups rich chicken stock made with extra onion, fresh coriander and lots of garlic

1 cup Fideos (small pasta shells), cooked or
   1 cup cooked rice or 1 cup cooked diced potatoes

1/4 teaspoon saffron
salt

freshly ground pepper

Heat stock and pasta, rice or potatoes. Stir in saffron and adjust seasonings with salt.
Pass the peppermill.
Serves 6
For a heartier meal add shredded tops of Chinese turnips (closest to vegetable available in Spain) and hunto* to taste.
*Hunto is a type of pork fat aged 6 or more months; it adds an unusual flavor. Sometimes available in Mexican markets.

## SOPA DE AJO

6 cups water
1 teaspoon salt
20 whole garlic cloves
2 teaspoons olive oil
4 beaten eggs
6 stale French bread slices

freshly ground pepper

Bring water, salt and garlic to boil and simmer 30 minutes. Remove garlic and add olive oil. Bring back to boil and gradually add eggs; let cook gently until eggs are set.
Add bread slices and let them soak up the broth. Serve immediately and pass the peppermill.
For true garlic lovers, add 5 pressed garlic cloves after the whole cloves have been removed.
Serves 6
Or ladle soup into 6 ovenproof bowls. Add a slice of bread fried in olive oil with garlic and onion and top each with a small egg. Bake in a preheated 375° oven until eggs are set.

## ESCUDELLA

1/2 cup garbanzo beans, soaked in water to
  cover 8 hours
1/2 cup small white beans
6 cups water
1 8-ounce ham hock
1 4-ounce piece lean pork
1 8-ounce lean short rib

3 pressed garlic cloves
1 onion, cut in 8ths
1 small whole cabbage, with bottom scored
  1/2 inch deep in 8ths
6 - 8 small whole potatoes

12 - 16 pilotas (see below)

salt
freshly ground pepper

*A garlicky main-meal soup!*

Combine garbanzo beans, white beans, water, ham
hock, pork and short rib. Cover, bring to boil and
cook 1-1/4 hours or until beans start to soften; add
water if needed.
Add garlic, onion, cabbage and potatoes; cook at
medium boil 5 minutes.
Add pilotas and cook 10 minutes.
Adjust seasonings with salt, adding boiling water if
needed to make 6 - 8 cups.
Remove cabbage and meat and place on platter to
be served with the soup.
Place 1 potato and 2 pilotas in each bowl and ladle
soup over. Serve with Spanish (French) bread and
pass the peppermill.
Serves 6 - 8

## PILOTAS

1/4 pound each ground beef and lean pork
1/2 teaspoon flour
1 pressed garlic clove
1 tablespoon finely minced parsley
1 teaspoon salt

1 beaten egg white

Combine meat, flour, garlic, parsley and salt. With
floured hands roll into 12 or 16 football-shaped
balls. Roll each ball in flour and then beaten egg
white.

## SOPA DE ARROZ

1/2 cup raw rice, well washed
3 cups water or stock
1/2 teaspoon salt
2 - 4 garlic cloves, pressed
2 teaspoons olive oil

*For the invalid—a recuperative soup*

Bring water or stock to boil with salt and garlic.
Add rice, bring back to boil, cover and simmer
15 minutes until rice is tender. Drizzle oil over,
cover and remove from heat. Let steep 5 minutes
without stirring.
Serves 3 - 4

## WINE GAZPACHO

2 pounds tomatoes, peeled, seeded and diced
1 cup minced onion
2 pressed garlic cloves
1/2 cup peeled, seeded and diced cucumber
1 3-1/4-ounce can pitted black olives, halved
4 drops Tabasco
1/2 teaspoon salt
1/4 teaspoon black pepper
1 tablespoon paprika
2 tablespoons olive oil
1/8 teaspoon sugar
1 cup dry red wine

extra diced vegetables
minced parsley
herb croutons

Combine ingredients and chill.
Adjust seasonings to taste, and serve in chilled bowls. Serve with extra diced vegetables, minced parsley and herb croutons.
Serves 6 - 8

## SPICY GAZPACHO

2 cups French bread cubes, soaked in
3 cups water
4 teaspoons minced garlic
1/2 cup minced onion
4 tomatoes, peeled and diced
3 tablespoons each olive oil and vinegar
1/2 teaspoon salt
1/4 teaspoon black pepper
6 drops Tabasco
1/8 teaspoon cumin

diced green tomato
cilantro sprigs

freshly ground pepper

Purée ingredients (except tomato dice and cilantro sprigs) in blender and chill.
Adjust seasonings and serve in chilled bowls; garnish with lots of diced green tomato and sprigs of cilantro.
Pass the peppermill.
Serves 4 - 6

## SOPA DE ALMENDRAS

1 tablespoon olive oil
1 tablespoon flour
2 cups chicken or veal stock

1 cup blanched almonds, ground
1/8 teaspoon each allspice and nutmeg
1/4 teaspoon thyme
1/4 teaspoon salt

2 cups milk

1/4 cup slivered almonds
1/2 teaspoon pimentón*

*see glossary

Heat oil, add flour and cook and stir 3 minutes. Gradually add stock; cook and stir until smooth and slightly thickened.
Add almonds and seasonings; cover, bring to boil and simmer gently 30 minutes.
Strain, forcing as much pulp through sieve as possible. Add milk, heat and adjust seasonings to taste. Garnish with slivered almonds that have been dusted with pimentón.
Serves 4 - 6
Good before a lamb dinner. Or serve as a luncheon soup with fruit salad and chicken sandwiches.

## SEAFOOD GAZPACHO

1-1/2 pounds mixed shellfish such as shrimp, lobster, langoustes and crab, cooked and diced or shredded
1 pressed garlic clove
1/4 cup olive oil
3 hard-cooked eggs
1/2 teaspoon dry mustard
1/4 cup lemon juice
5 cups tomato juice
2 tomatoes, peeled, seeded and minced
1/4 cup each finely minced bell pepper and red onion
1 large cucumber, peeled, seeded and minced
1/2 teaspoon Worcestershire sauce
3 drops Tabasco
1/2 teaspoon salt
1/4 teaspoon black pepper
1/16 teaspoon chili powder

minced parsley and chives
extra diced vegetables
garlic croutons

Mash garlic, oil, egg yolks, and mustard, stir in lemon juice and a cup or so of tomato juice; blend well and add rest of ingredients. Chill thoroughly. Adjust seasonings to taste and serve in chilled bowls sprinkled with minced parsley and chives.
Pass small dishes of extra minced tomato, cucumber, bell pepper, onion and hard-cooked egg white. Have lots of garlic croutons handy.
Serves 6 - 8

# Italian Soups

## MINESTRONE

This Italian classic of vegetables with pasta can be almost anything you wish to make it. With Italian or French bread and a light salad it often makes a full meal, though it needn't be that hearty. Some say never use smoked ham or bacon; others maintain such flavors are essential. The two recipes that follow are flexible and interchangeable. Use whatever is at hand.

## MINESTRONE WITH NAVY BEANS

1/3 cup navy beans
1 ham hock
1 whole garlic clove
1 small white onion
2 cups water

1/4 cup minced onion
1/2 cup minced leeks, white and some green
1 minced garlic clove
2 tablespoons olive oil

1/4 cup minced herbs (Italian parsley, basil,
   savory, rosemary, oregano, thyme and/or sage)

6 cups chicken, beef or veal stock
2 cups vegetables sliced (carrots, turnips, parsnips,
   green or wax beans, asparagus, peas, escarole,
   potatoes)

1/2 cup pasta

1 tablespoon tomato paste
1/2 teaspoon salt
1/4 teaspoon pepper
3/4 teaspoon dry mustard

crumbled blue or Gorgonzola cheese

Combine beans, ham hock, garlic, onion and water. Cover, bring to boil and simmer 1-1/2 - 2 hours until meat is tender, adding water as needed. Remove ham hock and cut meat into small pieces. Discard garlic and onion and set beans and their liquid aside.

Sauté onion, leeks and garlic in oil 5 minutes, add herbs and cook and stir a little longer to coat well. Add stock, bring to boil and add vegetables; cook 10 minutes or less, depending on which vegetables are used. Keep soup boiling, add beans, liquid, ham and pasta. Boil until pasta is tender.

Add tomato paste, salt, pepper and dry mustard. Adjust to taste and serve garnished with crumbled blue cheese or Gorgonzola.
Serves 6 - 8

## MINESTRONE WITH BASIL

2 slices bacon, diced
2 cups chopped onion

1/2 pound Italian sausage, chopped, browned
 and drained
8 cups beef stock
2 tablespoons minced fresh basil
1/2 cup minced Italian parsley
1 pressed garlic clove
1/4 teaspoon each cayenne pepper and
 black pepper
1 teaspoon salt
3 cups diced potatoes

1/2 cup soup pasta
4 cups loosely packed spinach leaves

croutons
grated Parmesan or Romano cheese

Sauté bacon and onion until golden. Add sausage, stock, basil, parsley, garlic, cayenne and pepper, salt and potatoes. Cover, bring to boil and cook 10 minutes.
Add soup pasta and cook 6 minutes. Add spinach, bring back to boil to just cook the spinach. Adjust seasonings to taste.
Serve with croutons and grated Parmesan or Romano cheese.
Serves 8 - 10

## ZUPPA MARITATA

1/4 cup minced green onions and tops
1/2 cup minced mushrooms
1 tablespoon olive oil
dash cayenne
1/4 teaspoon each salt and oregano
1 teaspoon lemon juice
6 cups rich chicken stock made with extra
 oregano and garlic

1/4 pound broken vermicelli

1 recipe cooked chicken balls (see page 179) or
1-1/2 cups diced cooked chicken

3 eggs, beaten
1 cup half-and-half cream
6 tablespoons grated Romano cheese

salt
pepper
oregano

paprika
minced Italian parsley
grated Romano cheese

Sauté green onions and mushrooms in oil until soft, sprinkling with cayenne, salt, oregano and lemon juice while cooking.
Add stock, bring to boil and stir in vermicelli; cook 7 minutes after the soup comes back to a boil.
Reheat with chicken balls or diced chicken.
Beat eggs and cream, whisk in 1/2 cup of hot soup and return to rest of soup. Heat but do not boil.
Add Romano cheese and adjust seasonings to taste with salt, pepper and oregano.
Sprinkle with paprika and minced Italian parsley and pass extra Romano cheese.
Serves 6

## ITALIAN ESCAROLE SOUP WITH MEATBALLS

1 pound marrow bones, sawed into 3-inch pieces
6 peppercorns
3 parsley sprigs
1 bay leaf
6 cups beef stock
1 teaspoon salt
2 tablespoons tomato paste

3/4 cup each diced onion, celery and carrot
1 cup diced potato

1 recipe Italian meatballs (see below)
3/4 pound escarole or Australian lettuce, shredded

minced parsley
grated Parmesan cheese

Combine bones, peppercorns, parsley, bay leaf, stock, salt and tomato paste. Cover, bring to boil and simmer 1 hour. Strain, cool, chill and defat.
Bring soup back to boil, add onion, celery and carrots and cook 10 minutes. Add potatoes and cook 5 more minutes.
Add meatballs and escarole and cook 10 minutes. Adjust seasonings.
Serve sprinkled with minced parsley. Pass grated Parmesan.
Serves 6 - 8

## ITALIAN MEATBALLS

3/4 cup ground round steak
1 egg
1 pressed garlic clove
3 tablespoons minced Italian parsley
1/2 teaspoon salt
1/4 teaspoon each pepper and oregano
1/2 - 1 teaspoon lemon juice
3 tablespoons grated Romano or Parmesan cheese

Mix ingredients, chill and form into small balls.

## ZUPPA ALLA VERMICELLI (WITH PILOU)

1/2 pound vermicelli, broken
2 tablespoons each butter and olive oil

1/2 cup minced onion
1 minced garlic clove

1 cup Italian tomatoes, or fresh tomatoes,
  peeled, seeded and minced

8 cups rich beef or chicken stock
1/2 cup minced Italian parsley

1/2 teaspoon salt
1/4 teaspoon black pepper

1 recipe pilou (see below)

grated Parmesan or Romano cheese

Sauté vermicelli in butter and oil, stirring, until golden. Remove with slotted spoon and reserve.
Add onion and garlic and sauté until soft.
Add tomatoes, stock, parsley and reserved vermicelli. Cover, bring to boil and cook until vermicelli is tender.
Adjust seasonings with salt and pepper and gradually pour over pilou in soup tureen.
Pass grated Parmesan or Romano cheese
Serves 8 - 10
Or add thinly sliced zucchini, cut beans, corn, peas or other vegetables at the same time as the vermicelli.

## PILOU

3 - 4 egg yolks
3 - 5 tablespoons olive oil

In soup tureen beat egg yolks until golden. Gradually add olive oil as if making mayonnaise, beating constantly, until smooth, but not as thick as mayonnaise.

## ZUPPA PAVESE

4 cups any rich stock

4 slices thick sour dough or Italian bread,
  fried in olive oil
4 small eggs

paprika
Italian parsley sprigs

Heat stock to boiling.
Place a slice of bread in each of 4 bowls, carefully break an egg onto each, and gradually pour hot soup over the egg to cook it slightly. (Poach the eggs first if you prefer them cooked solid.)
Serve with a sprinkle of paprika and Italian parsley sprigs.
Serves 4
Or pass grated Parmesan or Romano cheese.

## ZUPPA ALLA PISTOU

1 cup thinly sliced leeks, white only
1 cup celery, sliced thinly on diagonal
3/4 cup thinly sliced carrots
2 minced garlic cloves
2 tablespoons olive oil

6 cups rich beef, chicken or veal stock
1-1/2 cups green beans, cut on diagonal

1-1/2 cups diced potatoes
1 bunch spinach, chopped, or 1 package
  frozen chopped spinach, thawed
1 12-ounce can tomatoes, cut up
1/2 teaspoon thyme
1/4 teaspoon rosemary
1/2 teaspoon black pepper
3/4 teaspoon paprika
1-1/2 teaspoons salt

1-1/2 cups shredded iceberg lettuce
1 recipe pistou (see below)

grated Parmesan cheese

Sauté leeks, celery, carrots and garlic in oil until leeks are soft; do not brown. Add stock, bring to boil and add beans. Cook 5 minutes, add potatoes, spinach, tomatoes and seasonings, and bring back to boil. Cook 10 minutes until potatoes are almost tender. Add lettuce and boil 3 minutes until tender-crisp. Adjust seasonings.

Mix pistou in soup tureen, whisk in 1/2 cup of hot soup and gradually beat in rest of soup. Serve with grated Parmesan and extra pistou.

Serves 6 - 8

For heartier meal, add cooked red or white beans, pasta and other vegetables such as zucchini and mushrooms.

## PISTOU

1-1/2 teaspoons fresh basil
1 teaspoon minced garlic
1 tomato, peeled, seeded and diced or
  1 teaspoon tomato paste
1/4 cup grated Parmesan or Gruyère cheese
1/2 cup olive oil

Crush basil, garlic and tomato in mortar and transfer to soup tureen. Blend in cheese and gradually add olive oil, beating constantly.

# Oriental Soups

*An idealist is one who, on noticing that a rose smells better than a cabbage, concludes it will also make better soup.*

—*H. L. Mencken*

Volumes could be written about fascinating Oriental soups never encountered in restaurants. This I discovered under the tutelage of three experts, one Chinese, two Japanese. Especially interesting were the trips to Oriental markets to purchase fuzzy melon, dried fish stomach, seaweed, superior fresh seafoods and myriad other strange or familiar ingredients. Most Americans of European descent are just beginning to appreciate that weird (to them) odors of an Oriental market are far removed from the fragrant broths to be sipped from delicate bowls or centered on the table for individual ladling.

A common misconception is to think of foods of the Orient in terms of mostly Chinese or Japanese. Korea, Indochina, Indonesia, India, Ceylon and other Far East countries have many tasty foods and flavors, too.

For those fortunate enough to live in an area with Oriental neighborhoods, it's easy to build up a supply of dried items for variety in many dishes. They keep indefinitely and need only to be thoroughly washed before using, sometimes soaked to soften. For those interested in experimenting and unable to purchase in their area, write for information on direct mail to P.O. Box 1074, San Rafael, California, 94901.

Dried forest mushrooms must *always* be soaked. Cover with lukewarm water for 10 minutes or more, rinse, dry and use as recipe directs. For Japanese recipes, sprinkle with a little sugar when soaking.

The light soy is less salty than the heavier, dark variety and is to be used in all recipes.

For the more complicated Oriental soups soaking, dicing and other preliminary processing of ingredients should be done well ahead of time. You'll note that some of the soups can be prepared the day before. Refrigerate, and reheat just before serving—a great help to cooks who are also hosts or hostesses.

# INDONESIAN FISH BALL SOUP

6 cups fish stock

1 cup celery, sliced thinly on diagonal

1 recipe fish balls (see below)

3 ounces bean-thread noodles*, soaked 10 minutes, drained and cut into 5-inch lengths

1/2 teaspoon salt

1/4 teaspoon pepper

nutmeg

slivered green onions

lemon slices

*see glossary

*Indonesian cooking has taken ingredients from the Chinese and Japanese; thus the bean-thread noodles.*

Combine stock and celery; cover, bring to boil and simmer 10 minutes.

Keep at slow boil and add fish balls; cook 5 minutes or until balls rise to top.

Add bean-thread noodles, salt, pepper and nutmeg. Bring back to boil and cook 2 minutes. Adjust seasonings and serve with slivered green onions and lemon slices.

Serves 6

Or add peeled, diced winter melon at the same time as the fish balls.

# FISH BALLS

1/2 pound filet of sole, ground

1 teaspoon cornstarch

1/2 teaspoon salt

1/4 teaspoon nutmeg

1 teaspoon melted butter

Mix ingredients, chill and form into small balls.

## INDONESIAN BEEF BROTH WITH MEATBALLS

6 cups beef stock
2 bay leaves
1 teaspoon Laos*
1 teaspoon Serehpoeder*
1/2 teaspoon garlic powder

1/2 cup celery, thinly sliced on diagonal
1 teaspoon vegetable oil
1 recipe meatballs (see below)

salt
pepper

slivered green onions

*see glossary

Combine stock, bay leaf and seasonings. Cover, bring to boil and simmer gently 30 minutes to blend flavors. Remove bay leaves.
Sauté celery in oil, covered, 10 minutes. Add to broth, bring to gentle boil and drop in as many meatballs as desired. Cook 8 - 10 minutes and adjust seasonings to taste with salt and pepper. Serve with lots of slivered green onions.
Serves 6

## MEATBALLS

1/4 pound each ground round steak and
  lean pork butt
1/2 cup mashed potatoes made without butter or
  seasoning (instant is fine)
1/2 teaspoon soy sauce
1/4 teaspoon salt
1/8 teaspoon each mace and nutmeg
1 tablespoon cornstarch

Mix ingredients thoroughly, form balls the size of marbles and chill at least 1 hour. Freeze or use in soup. Can also cook in boiling salted water.

# INDONESIAN CHICKEN BROTH

6 cups chicken stock
2 bay leaves
1/2 teaspoon Laos*
1/2 teaspoon Serehpoeder*
1/2 teaspoon Boemboe Godok*
1/2 teaspoon garlic powder
1 slice fresh ginger root

3/4 cup celery, thinly sliced on diagonal
1/2 cup diced onion
2 teaspoons oil

2 - 3 ounces bean-thread noodles*, soaked in
    water to cover 10 minutes, drained and
    cut into 4-inch lengths

1 cup raw chicken julienne

slivered green onions

*see glossary

Combine stock, bay leaves, ginger, and seasonings. Cover, bring to boil and simmer 30 minutes. Add chicken last 10 minutes. Remove bay leaves and ginger.
Sauté celery and onion in oil, covered, 10 minutes. Add to broth, bring to boil and cook 5 minutes.
Add bean-thread noodles and boil 2 - 3 minutes.
Adjust seasonings to taste.
Sprinkle with slivered green onions.
Serves 6

## CURRIED EGGPLANT SOUP

1 tablespoon olive oil
1 cup cubed, unpeeled eggplant

1/4 cup minced green onions and tops
1/2 teaspoon minced garlic
1 tablespoon butter
4 teaspoons flour
1 - 2 teaspoons curry powder
2 cups milk
1/4 teaspoon each crushed rosemary and oregano

1/2 cup heavy cream
salt
pepper

Sauté eggplant in oil until golden. In saucepan, sauté onion and garlic until onion is soft. Sprinkle with flour and curry, cook and stir 3 minutes and gradually add milk. Cook and stir until thickened, add rosemary, oregano and eggplant. Simmer 15 minutes. Force through sieve, leaving peel behind.
Heat, add cream and reheat; do not boil. Adjust seasonings with salt and pepper.
Serves 3 - 4

## CURRIED TURKEY

6 cups rich turkey stock
1 cup chopped onion
3/4 cup diced, peeled tart apple
2 teaspoons curry powder
1/4 teaspoon cardamon
1/2 teaspoon salt

3 egg yolks, beaten
1 cup buttermilk
1/4 teaspoon garlic powder
1 cup cubed cooked turkey

minced parsley
crisp bacon bits
almonds sautéed in butter

Simmer stock, onion, apple, curry, cardamon and salt 1/2 hour. Purée in blender.
Beat yolks, buttermilk and garlic powder and add to stock with cooked turkey. Bring just to boil, adjust seasonings to taste and sprinkle with lots of minced parsley.
Pass crisp bacon bits and almonds sautéed in butter.
Serves 6

## CEYLONESE CONSOMMÉ

3 cups pared, diced tart apples
3/4 cup minced onion
1 cup chopped celery leaves
3 tablespoons sweet butter
1 - 2 teaspoons curry powder

3 10-1/2-ounce cans consommé
1 soup can water

3 cups half-and-half cream

*Wonderful to serve in the living room as a cocktail-stopper.*

Sauté apple, onion and celery leaves in butter 10 minutes; do not brown. Sprinkle with curry; cook and stir 3 minutes.
Add consommé and water, bring to boil and simmer, uncovered, 15 minutes. Strain and adjust seasonings.
Add cream and reheat. Needs no garnish.
Serves 6 - 8
May be served cold.

## CREAMY CEYLONESE SOUP WITH CURRY PUFFS

1-1/2 cups pared, diced apples
3 tablespoons grated onion
2 tablespoons butter
1 tablespoon flour
1 - 2 teaspoons curry powder

4-1/2 cups chicken stock
1/2 cup dry white wine

3 egg yolks, beaten
2 cups heavy cream

3/4 cup minced, cooked chicken or shrimp

salt
white pepper
half-and-half cream

minced chives or minced green onion tops

1 recipe curry puffs

Sauté apple and onion in butter 10 minutes without browning. Sprinkle with flour and curry; cook and stir 3 minutes.
Gradually add stock and wine; cook and stir until smooth and slightly thickened. Cover and cook gently 20 minutes. Strain and reheat.
Beat yolks and cream, whisk in 1/2 cup hot soup and return to rest of soup. Cook and stir 3 minutes without boiling. Cool and chill.
Adjust seasonings with salt and pepper, thin with half-and-half cream if desired, and sprinkle with chicken or shrimp. Serve in chilled bowls and garnish with minced chives or green onion tops. Pass curry puffs.
Serves 6 - 8
If served hot, garnish with sieved hard-cooked eggs and paprika.

## CURRY PUFFS

1 1-pound package phyllo*

1 pound ground beef

3 tablespoons butter
1/4 cup minced onion
1/8 teaspoon garlic powder
1/2 - 1 teaspoon cumin
1 teaspoon salt
dash cinnamon, ginger powder and cayenne

1/2 cup yoghurt

1/2 cup minced cooked potato
1 chopped hard-cooked egg
1/2 cup raisins
1 tablespoon lemon juice

Sauté beef until brown, remove from pan and drain. Pour any remaining fat from pan, add butter and sauté onions until soft.

Add seasonings, return meat to pan, cook and stir 3 minutes.

Blend in yoghurt and simmer to absorb almost all the liquid.

Add remaining ingredients, mix well and cool.

When working with phyllo pastry always keep it covered with wax paper and a dampened towel to prevent drying. If the layers break, don't worry, as you can "mend" them with the melted butter as you place layer on layer. Remove 4 layers at a time, spread each with melted butter using a pastry brush, and restack them. Cut into 2-1/2-inch rounds, place 1 teaspoon of filling on rounds and fold over to form a half-moon shape, crimping the edges to seal. Place on cooky sheet and repeat until all the filling is used, making about 30 puffs. Bake in a 350° oven 15 minutes or until golden.

Any leftover pastry can be used for strudel, baklava, or even a casing for meat loaf. Wrap well and refrigerate up to 5 days.

*Phyllo pastry sheets are available in pound packages in Armenian or Greek specialty shops and in many delicatessens. I do not recommend frozen phyllo, but if none other is available be sure to let it defrost overnight in the refrigerator before using.

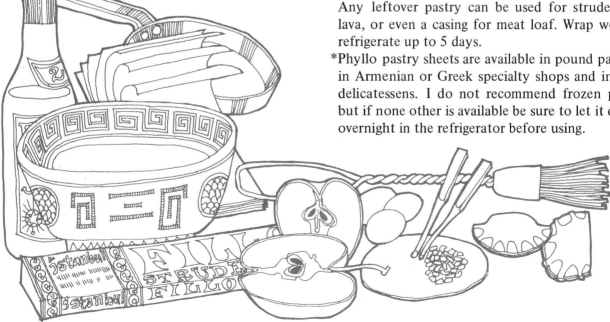

## THE ORIENTAL FIREPOT

Strangers become friends and friends get friendlier around an intimate firepot soup. The shiny brass firepot filled with glowing charcoal designed specifically for this soup is spectacular, though not absolutely necessary. Electric casserole cookers or pretty kettles over braziers make suitable substitutes.

The seafood, poultry, meat, vegetables and garnishes and seasonings listed are just a few of many you may wish to try. Arrange them attractively on platters and trays where they'll be easily accessible to you and your guests. Surround the pot with individual plates and bowls. The broth should be gently simmering. Everyone picks up his chopsticks and cooks morsels in the broth. Keeping track of whose morsels are whose can be quite a game.

Small individual sieves are best for retrieving the morsels at their parboiled, crunchy best. The retrieved delicacies may be eaten with chopsticks or sandwiched in pieces of iceberg lettuce. It's advisable to provide Oriental soup spoons, too, for sipping the broth later.

If desired, each guest may break a small egg into his bowl, beat it lightly and dip hot morsels into it before or after seasoning.

When everyone has had his fill of morsels, add bean-thread noodles and 2 beaten eggs to broth; let simmer to set eggs and serve. Or omit beaten eggs and ladle hot soup over eggs left in bowls.

8 cups basic Chinese chicken stock (see page 75)

8 halved scallops
8 shrimp, halved lengthwise
1 small abalone, cut in julienne
1 filet of sole, cubed
other firm raw fish in season

1 chicken breast, cut in julienne
1 pork filet, cut in julienne
1/2 pound top sirloin beef, thinly sliced
3 chicken gizzards, scored and thinly sliced

1 bunch small spinach leaves
1 small Chinese cabbage, pulled apart
1 bunch watercress sprigs
4 green onions, cut in 4-inch pieces
other vegetables in season

4 ounces bean-thread noodles*, soaked 10 minutes
  and cut into 6-inch lengths

*In small bowls*

hoisin sauce*
mustard
slivered green onions
toasted sesame seeds

*In attractive shake bottles*

soy sauce
dry sherry
sesame oil
oyster sauce*
white vinegar

aji oil*

eggs

*see glossary

## KOOK WITH MANDOO

1/2 pound round steak, cut on diagonal
  into very thin slices
3 minced green onions
2 tablespoons soy sauce
1/2 teaspoon minced garlic
1/2 teaspoon peeled and minced fresh ginger root
1/2 teaspoon toasted sesame seeds

1-1/2 tablespoons corn oil

4 cups water
2 cups beef stock
1 large dried forest mushroom, softened

12 pea pods, blanched 2 minutes
1 small square tofu*, diced
1 recipe mandoo (see below)
slivered green onions

*see glossary

Marinate meat with green onions, soy, garlic, ginger
and sesame seeds at least 2 hours.
Heat oil and frizzle meat to brown.
Add water, stock and mushroom. Cover, bring to
boil and simmer 20 minutes. Remove mushroom
and cut into 12 slivers; set aside.
Adjust seasoning with salt.
Arrange 2 mushroom slivers, 2 pea pods, several
tofu dice and as many mandoo as desired in
6 bowls. Ladle soup over and sprinkle with slivered
green onions.
Serves 6

## MANDOO

1/2 pound ground round steak
2 tablespoons Kim Chee*, drained,
  squeezed dry and chopped
1/4 cup bean sprouts, blanched, drained,
  squeezed dry and chopped
1 tablespoon minced green onions
1/2 teaspoon finely minced fresh ginger root

1 teaspoon toasted sesame seeds
1/8 teaspoon each pepper, paprika and sugar
1/2 teaspoon salt
1 teaspoon cornstarch
wonton skins (see page 77)

*see glossary

Mix ingredients, fill wonton skins as directed in
wonton soup, and cook in boiling salted water
5 minutes or until they rise to the surface.

## ORIENTAL CRAB & CORN BISQUE

8 cups basic Chinese chicken or
  pork stock (see page 75)
6 fresh mushrooms, sliced, or
6 dried forest mushrooms, softened and slivered
1 white onion, sliced
2 cups  white cream-style corn

sugar
soy sauce
pepper
1 - 1-1/2 cups flaked crab meat

2 eggs, beaten

Chinese parsley sprigs

Simmer stock, mushrooms and onion 30 minutes, adding corn last 10 minutes, keeping at a slow boil. Adjust seasonings with sugar, soy and pepper, add crab and reheat.
Bring to slow boil and gradually drizzle in eggs. Remove from heat and serve immediately. Garnish with Chinese parsley sprigs.
Serves 8

## THAI SOUP WITH LEMON

1/2 pound fish heads and scraps
3/4 pound raw shrimp
2 bay leaves
6 peppercorns
1 sliced onion
tops of 4 green onions, chopped
3 tablespoons lemon juice
1 tablespoon lemon rind
6 cups water

1/2 pound lean pork cut in julienne
1 raw chicken breast, cut in julienne

1/2 pound firm white fish filet,
  cut into 1-inch squares

fish sauce, fish soy*
lemon juice
salt

*see glossary

Shell and devein shrimp, dice and reserve. Combine shells, fish heads and scraps, bay leaves, peppercorns, onion, green onion tops, lemon juice and rind and water. Cover, bring to boil and simmer 30 minutes; skim off any scum that rises to surface. Strain and reheat. Add pork and cook 10 minutes; add chicken and cook 5 minutes. Bring back to boil, add fish squares and cook gently 5 more minutes. Add shrimp dice, bring back to boil and remove from heat.
Season to taste with fish sauce or fish soy, lemon juice and salt.
Serves 6 - 8.

Although appearance is important in Chinese cooking, and many of their foods look really spectacular, flavor and texture are even more important.

- When one vegetable or meat is diced, all others in recipe should be diced whenever possible; if slivered, all slivered.
- A dash of sugar often brings out just the flavor you're looking for.
- Soy sauce will darken soup and ingredients, so if you want to keep fish, tofu, chicken and water chestnuts white, let your guests add soy.
- The Chinese like Virginia ham and it is usually available in their markets. Substitute proscuitto, sliced 1/4-inch thick.
- Ingredients can be omitted, increased, or decreased in Chinese soups more than any others. Keep a varied stock on hand for exploring the possibilities.
- Ginger need not be peeled. Just slice, wash and use to flavor.
- There is no substitute for dried tangerine which can be purchased in Chinese markets; sometimes called dried orange peel.
- Rice should be long grain. I prefer the brands from Texas.

# Chinese Soups

## BASIC CHINESE BROTH

1 pound raw chicken or pork bones
8 cups water
1 - 2 slices fresh ginger root
dash sugar
salt

*This broth is to be used in all Chinese soups.*

Combine chicken and/or pork bones with water and ginger; cover, bring to boil, skim off any scum that rises to top, and simmer gently 45 minutes to 1-1/2 hours. Strain and season to taste with sugar and salt.

## VARIATIONS: CHINESE BROTH

- Cut Chinese cabbage lengthwise, wash and slice. Add to broth and simmer 10 minutes.
- Add 1 cup diced tofu (see glossary) to broth and simmer 5 minutes.
- Combine the cabbage and tofu in the broth.
- Add dried forest mushrooms, softened and slivered, to broth and simmer 20 minutes.
- Cut core end of mustard greens in 1/2-inch slices, cut green part into 2-inch slices; cover with water and wash thoroughly in several changes of water. Drain and add to boiling pork stock that has simmered with an extra slice of ginger root. Bring to boil and cook 5 minutes. Remove ginger and adjust seasonings.

## WONTON SOUP

6 cups basic Chinese chicken or pork broth
  (see page 75)
1 strand dried turnip greens (optional)*,
  washed to remove sand
1 dried tangerine peel*, soaked 10 minutes
4 dried forest mushrooms, softened and slivered

salt

soy sauce

24 wontons (see page 77)

Chinese parsley sprigs

*see glossary

Simmer broth with turnip greens, tangerine peel and mushrooms for 30 minutes. Remove greens and tangerine peel. Season to taste with salt and soy. Keep hot.

In separate saucepan cook wontons in salted boiling water 4 - 5 minutes until they rise to top; do not boil too hard. Then cook 1 more minute and drain well.

Remove wontons with slotted spoon and place 4 in each of 6 bowls. Fill bowls with hot soup and garnish with Chinese parsley sprigs.
Serves 6

## WAH WONTON SOUP

6 cups broth treated as above
3 chicken gizzards, scored and thinly sliced
3 chicken hearts, sliced
1/2 cup slivered bamboo shoots
3 chicken livers, halved or quartered
3 medium squid, cleaned, halved, and scored lightly
  before slicing bodies and cutting up tentacles
1/4 pound pea pods or 1 small bunch bok choy,
  coarsely chopped and well washed
6 shrimp, cleaned and halved lengthwise

24 - 48 wontons (see page 77)

Bring simmered broth to boil, add gizzards and hearts and cook 3 minutes. Add bamboo shoots, livers, squid and vegetable; bring back to boil and cook 2 minutes. Add shrimp, bring just to boil and remove from heat. Add wontons, as in wonton soup.
Serves 6 - 8
Or can add pieces of cooked slivered pork and/or chicken, and for a main meal more wontons.

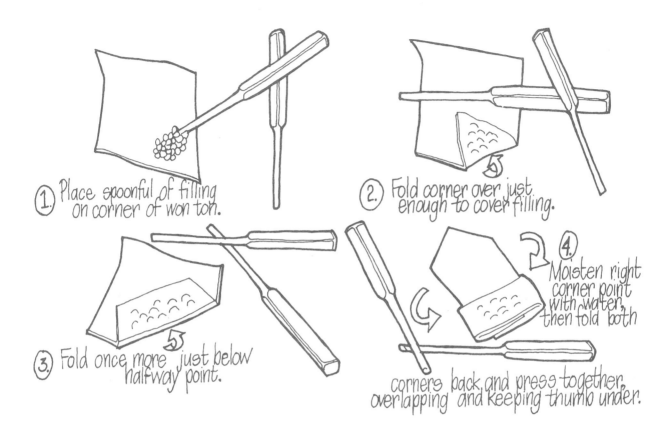

1. Place spoonful of filling on corner of won ton.

2. Fold corner over just enough to cover filling.

3. Fold once more just below halfway point.

4. Moisten right corner point with water, then fold both corners back and press together, overlapping and keeping thumb under.

## WONTONS

Ready-made wonton skins, in 1-pound packages of squares or rounds, are sold in many markets other than Oriental. There are about 80 in each package, depending upon how thin they've been rolled. If well wrapped, they may be frozen, but the skins dry out more readily and become difficult to manipulate.

Homemade skins are equally as good, but without proper equipment it is difficult to roll them thin enough. The recipe follows in case you can't find them in your market.

1/2 cup hot water
1 teaspoon each salad oil and salt
2 cups flour

Combine hot water, oil and salt; quickly add flour, mix well and knead until smooth.

Roll into 3 or 4 1/2-inch ropes, wrap each in wax paper and refrigerate 30 minutes.

Working with one rope at a time, cut off 1/2-inch slices and roll as thinly as possible into squares or rounds.

Stack, keeping covered, and repeat with remaining ropes.

This recipe makes about 40 skins.

## SHRIMP WONTON FILLING

1 pound raw shrimp, cleaned and
  ground or finely minced
1/2 cup minced water chestnuts (canned)
1 tablespoon minced green onions
1/4 teaspoon garlic powder
1/2 teaspoon salt
1 teaspoon soy sauce
1 teaspoon sake or dry sherry
1 tablespoon cornstarch

Mix ingredients thoroughly and fill wonton squares
as directed.

## PORK & SHRIMP WONTON FILLING

1/2 pound ground lean pork butt
1/2 pound raw shrimp, cleaned and ground
  or finely minced
1 tablespoon minced Chinese parsley
3 minced green onions and tops
1 tablespoon soy sauce
8 minced water chestnuts (canned)
1/2 teaspoon salt
1 tablespoon cornstarch
1 egg, beaten

Mix ingredients thoroughly and fill wonton squares
as directed.

## BEEF WONTON FILLING

1 pound ground beef
2 tablespoons minced green onion
1 minced garlic clove
2 teaspoons sake or dry sherry
1 tablespoon cornstarch
1 tablespoon soy sauce
1 teaspoon salt
1/4 teaspoon grated fresh ginger root

Mix ingredients thoroughly. Place 1 rounded teaspoon of filling in center of round wontons, fold
over to make half-moon shape and crimp edges,
using water to seal.
These wontons will be larger than the preceding
recipes for wonton squares.

## PORK WONTON FILLING

3/4 pound minced lean pork butt
2 tablespoons minced green onions
1 minced garlic clove
2 teaspoons sake or dry sherry
1 tablespoon soy sauce
1 teaspoon salt

Mix ingredients thoroughly and fill wonton
squares as directed.

# SEAWEED SOUP

8 cups Chinese chicken or pork broth
  (see page 75)
4 dried forest mushrooms, softened and slivered
1 slice fresh ginger root
1/4 cup dried shrimp**

1 handful of dried, bulk seaweed*, soaked in cold
  water 10 minutes, washed in three or four
  changes of water, and coarsely chopped
1/2 cup ground pork
1/4 cup diced water chestnuts (canned)

1/4 cup chopped green onions

*6 sheets of seaweed may be substituted for the bulk
 seaweed, but bulk is tastier and has a better texture
 (see glossary).

**see glossary

Combine stock, mushrooms, ginger and shrimp;
cover, bring to boil and simmer 20 minutes.
Add seaweed, pork and water chestnuts; bring to
boil and simmer 15 minutes.
Just before serving sprinkle with green onions.
Serves 6 - 8
Can beat in 1 beaten egg at last minute; or add 1
cup diced tofu (see glossary) or 1/2 cup diced raw
shrimp; bring just to boil.

## DICED WINTER MELON SOUP

8 cups basic Chinese chicken or
  pork broth (see page 75)
2 pounds winter melon, washed, peeled and diced
6 large dried forest mushrooms, softened and diced
1 1-inch piece dried tangerine peel*, soaked
  10 minutes
1/2 cup each diced water chestnuts (canned)
  and diced bamboo shoots
1 raw chicken breast, diced

salt

1/2 cup Virginia ham, cut in slivers
Chinese parsley sprigs

*see glossary

Combine broth, winter melon, mushrooms, tangerine peel, water chestnuts and bamboo shoots in
large kettle; cover, bring to boil, and simmer gently
1 hour, adding chicken dice last 10 minutes.
Discard tangerine peel and adjust seasonings with
salt.
Garnish with ham and Chinese parsley.
Serves 8 - 10
Or add 1/2 cup frozen peas, bring just to boil and
add 2 tablespoons dry sherry just before serving.

## WINTER MELON POND SOUP

Instead of using diced winter melon, the broth,
mushrooms, tangerine peel, water chestnuts, bamboo shoots and chicken are cooked in the whole
melon and the soup is served from the melon—a
spectacular dish!
Buy an evenly shaped melon, about 10 pounds in
weight; cut 1/4 off top and set aside. Scrape out the
pulp and seeds and set the melon in a bowl that just
fits its circumference. Make a string "harness"
around bowl and melon, or wrap in double-strength
cheesecloth, for easy handling; set on a rack in a
large kettle. Fill the melon with stock and ingredients, saving any extra stock to serve later. Put top
on melon and pour boiling water into kettle, filling
7/8th full. Cover kettle and steam gently 3 hours.
Lift melon and bowl from kettle, remove harness or
cheesecloth, discard tangerine peel, and serve,
scooping out some of the flesh with each serving.
Add canned, drained and sliced abalone heated in a
little stock, if desired.

## FUZZY MELON SOUP

1 fuzzy melon (about 1/2 pound)

6 cups Chinese chicken or pork stock (see page 75)
1 tablespoon dried shrimp*

1 egg, beaten

Chinese parsley

*see glossary

## QUICK WATERCRESS SOUP

4 cups water
1/4 pound ground lean pork butt
1 slice fresh ginger root
1/2 teaspoon salt
1/4 cup diced water chestnuts (canned)

2 bunches watercress, large stems removed
 (1 quart loosely packed)

1 cup diced tofu*

*see glossary

*A light, before-dinner broth with a delicate flavor that cannot be duplicated.*

Scrape fuzz off melon and cut into bite-size slices. Simmer stock and shrimp 20 minutes. Bring stock back to boil, add melon, and cook 5 minutes after stock returns to boil.
Drizzle egg into soup and cook 2 minutes.
Garnish with Chinese parsley.
Serves 6

Bring water to boil, crumble in pork, and add ginger, salt and water chestnuts. Cook at gentle boil 15 minutes.
Bring to hard boil, add watercress and cook 5 minutes.
Add tofu and cook 3 minutes.
Serves 4 - 6
For easier eating cut up large watercress sprigs.

## GOEY GAW

1-1/2 ounces goey gaw*, soaked 1 hour
 in cold water, turning often

10 cups Chinese chicken stock (see page 75)
1 slice fresh ginger root
1 piece dried tangerine peel*
1 raw chicken breast, sliced

1/2 pound pea pods

*see glossary

*The idea of fish stomach may not appeal to
everyone, but the texture is marvelous and the
flavor of the soup delicate.*

Cut goey gaw down center and then cut into
1-inch dice. Set aside.
Simmer stock, ginger and tangerine peel 20 minutes.
Bring soup to boil, add goey gaw and chicken,
bring back to boil and cook 10 minutes.
Add pea pods, bring back to boil and immediately remove from heat.
Serves 8

## CHINESE OXTAIL — BLACK BEAN SOUP

1 whole lean oxtail, about 1-1/2 pounds,
 cut into 1-1/2-inch lengths, large pieces halved

8 cups water
1 washed dried tangerine peel*
8 - 10 dried mushrooms, softened
8 - 10 jujubes*, washed, not soaked
1 slice fresh ginger root
3/4 teaspoon salt
1/2 teaspoon sugar

1 cup black beans, washed and blanched,
 rinsed and then soaked in water to cover
 3 - 4 hours

*see glossary

Blanch oxtails and combine with water, tangerine
peel, mushrooms, jujubes, ginger, salt and sugar.
Cover, bring to boil and simmer 1-1/2 hours.
Add beans and cook 1/2 - 1 hour longer until beans
are tender but still hold their shape. Remove tanger-
ine peel and adjust seasonings to taste.
Soup is clear because beans have been blanched.
Serves 8 - 10
Can add 1 teaspoon whiskey or dry sherry to each
bowl when serving.

# CHINESE CHICKEN WHISKEY SOUP

1-1/2 pounds chicken wings or other cut
  of choice

2 ounces dried black fungus*, soaked in
  warm water 10 minutes
1/2 cup dried needles*, soaked
  5 minutes in cold water to soften
10 small dried forest mushrooms, softened
1 cup blanched, raw Virginia peanuts

3 tablespoons corn oil
1/2 teaspoon salt
5 - 8 slices fresh ginger root

3 cups boiling water
1/4 cup bourbon

*see glossary

*This is served to Chinese mothers after their babies are born to help them regain their strength. It makes an excellent after-theater soup. Better made the day ahead and reheated. The needles add an unusual sweet flavor.*

Remove tips from wings and reserve for future stock. Cut wings at joint and set aside.
Cut out any hard membrane in fungus and pull apart into bite-size pieces. Set aside. Tie each needle into a knot and set aside.
Heat oil, sprinkle with salt and sauté ginger 2 minutes over high heat. Add wings and brown. Add fungus, mushrooms and peanuts; cook and stir over high heat 1 minute.
Cover with boiling water, add bourbon, cover, bring to boil and simmer 20 minutes, adding needles last 10 minutes of cooking. Just before serving skim off surface fat.
Serves 6

# LOTUS ROOT SOUP

8 cups Chinese chicken or pork broth
  (see page 75)
1 strand dried turnip greens (optional)*, well
  washed to remove sand
5 - 6 dried lotus roots*, soaked in water to
  cover 2 hours and halved or quartered, or
1 pound fresh lotus root, scraped and sliced
4 jujubes*, soaked in water to cover until soft
1 dried tangerine peel*, soaked 10 minutes
4 - 6 dried forest mushrooms, softened
  and slivered

*see glossary

Slice jujubes, discarding pit; combine with rest of
ingredients and broth; cover kettle and bring to
boil.
Simmer gently 2 hours.
Remove tangerine peel and turnip green.
Serves 8 - 10

# SIZZLING RICE SOUP

1 cup well-washed rice
1-1/2 cups water

6 cups chicken stock
1 cup sliced button mushrooms (canned)
1/4 cup sliced water chestnuts (canned)
1/2 cup diagonally sliced bamboo shoots
1 raw chicken breast, cut in julienne

2 cups shredded lettuce or Chinese cabbage

corn oil

*The sizzle's the secret; don't muff it. Cooking rice
the Chinese way is essential.*

Combine rice and water in heavy frying pan and let
stand at least 1 hour. Bring to boil, uncovered, over
high heat, lower heat slightly and boil until water
evaporates.
Cover with a tight lid, reduce heat to its lowest and
cook 1-1/2 hours or until the crust that has formed
can be removed easily from pan.
Refrigerate 1 hour or more and break into bite-size
pieces.
Bring stock to boil, add mushrooms, water chestnuts, bamboo shoots and chicken. Cook 10 minutes, add lettuce or cabbage and bring back to boil.
Cook 1 minute.
While soup is cooking, deep fry rice pieces in corn
oil until golden. Drain on paper toweling and keep
hot in a casserole in a 375° oven.
The timing is important—both the fried rice and the
soup should be very hot. Bring the casserole to the
table and let your guests watch you pour the soup
over it and enjoy the sizzle. Also the taste!

## YUON WINTER SOUP
## STICKY RICE FLOUR BALL SOUP

8 cups Chinese chicken or pork stock (see page 75)
  cooked with 1 1-inch piece dried tangerine peel**
  and 1 strand well-washed dried turnip green**

1 1-1/2-pound Chinese turnip*, scraped and
  cut into julienne
10 dried forest mushrooms, softened and slivered
3 tablespoons dried shrimp** (optional)
3 - 4 Lop Chiang**, sliced on diagonal

1/4 pound lean pork butt, ground once
dash sesame oil
1 tablespoon each soy sauce and cornstarch
1/2 teaspoon salt

2 teaspoons grated fresh orange rind

1 recipe rice flour balls (see below)


*Chinese turnips are a winter vegetable; use Chinese
cabbage instead if desired, adding last 15 minutes of
cooking.

**see glossary

*To be served as a hearty, cold-weather main meal.
Very rich in vitamin B because of the rice flour.
The balls have a chewy texture; try more than one
before you decide whether or not you like them.*

Combine stock, tangerine peel, turnip green, turnip
julienne, mushrooms and shrimp. Cover, bring to
boil and simmer 30 minutes.
Mix pork, sesame oil, soy sauce, cornstarch and salt.
Bring soup back to boil, add Lop Chiang slices and
pork mixture a teaspoonful at a time; cook
10 minutes.
Discard tangerine peel and dried turnip, taste for
salt and just before serving add orange rind.
Place 4 or 5 rice flour balls in each of 8 - 10 bowls,
pour soup over and garnish with slivered green
onions.


## RICE FLOUR BALLS

1-1/2 cups glutinous Chinese rice flour
1/2 cup hot water

While broth is simmering, make balls or make ahead
and store in plastic bag with extra rice flour to
prevent sticking.
Measure 1 cup rice flour into bowl and drizzle very
hot water over, stirring constantly with chopsticks
or fork. Mix thoroughly and then knead until
smooth. Roll into 1/2-inch thick ropes, pinch off
1/2-inch pieces and roll into small balls.
Just before soup is ready drop balls into boiling
salted water; keep at boil until balls rise to surface
and become puffy.

## JOOK (CHINESE THICK RICE SOUP-CONGEE)

8 cups rich turkey broth made from leftover
  cooked turkey carcass
8 dried forest mushrooms, softened and slivered
1 large piece dried tangerine peel*
1/2 dried, well-washed turnip green*, sliced

1 cup raw rice, not washed
2-1/2 cups boiling water

3 - 4 sheets dried sheet tofu*, broken into
  bite-size pieces

1 - 2 cups diced leftover turkey
3 Lop Chiang*, sliced on diagonal

sesame oil
soy
salt

slivered green onions
Chinese parsley sprigs
raw fish slices

*see glossary

*Never as a first course—good as a main meal, or for a late supper or breakfast. Bland and interesting. Cold-weather soup. Can be made ahead and reheated over and over again.*

Simmer broth, mushrooms, tangerine peel and turnip green while making rice.

Over high heat cook rice in boiling water, stirring occasionally. Keep a teakettle of boiling water ready to add as needed. After 15 minutes lower heat slightly. Rice should cook until it is completely broken up and gooey, 30 to 40 minutes.

Add rice to broth, cook and stir occasionally for 1 hour or until broth resembles a gruel. Last 15 minutes add tofu; last 10 minutes add turkey and sausages. Keep adding boiling water as needed. Adjust seasonings with sesame oil, soy and salt. Pass bowls of slivered green onions and Chinese parsley sprigs. Serve with raw fish slices to dip into hot soup.

Serves 8 - 10

Or use chicken or pork stock, add pork balls, garnish with shredded iceberg lettuce and serve with raw marinated beef slices in each bowl.

# Japanese Soups

Delicacy of flavor, beautiful and artistic garnishes, graceful bowls and ritualistic serving characterize Japanese soups, which are second only to rice in culinary importance. Odd numbers are considered lucky in Japan; even numbers unlucky. Thus the Japanese place odd numbers of each type of morsel in the bowl and odd numbers of people are seated around the table. Bowls are sold in sets of five, not six.

The three major types of soup are:
• *Suimono:* clear, served at the beginning of the meal.
• *Miso:* thickened with crushed and fermented soy beans and served towards the end of a meal or for breakfast.
• *Sumashi-shiru:* main-meal soup like either of the above, only with higher proportions of solids to be served along with rice.
Dashi is the base of all three types. The hot soup often serves to heat the morsels, so whenever possible cover the bowls immediately.

# SUIMONO (BASIC DASHI)

## Dashi #1

6 cups water
1 6-inch by 2-inch piece kombu*
1-1/2 cups katsuobushi*
1/8 teaspoon sugar
1/2 teaspoon salt

*see glossary

Break kombu into several pieces, combine with rest of ingredients, bring to boil and cook rapidly 3 minutes. Do not overcook. Strain and reserve kombu and katsuobushi.

## Dashi #2

Repeat recipe, using reserved kombu and katsuobushi; boil 5 minutes. This increases the strength of the flavor.

## VARIATIONS (DASHI #1 OR #2)

• In salted water parboil 1 shrimp per person (cleaned, tail left on) and 3 pea pods per person. Place in bowl, add dashi and garnish with tiny lemon peel strip.
• Boil 1 or 3 clams per person in dashi until they open. Garnish with minced chives or green onion tops.
• Place 1 or 3 small squares raw filet of sole or striped bass in bowl. Pour hot dashi over and garnish with tiny lemon peel strip.
• In salted water, parboil slices of fresh mushroom and somen (thin noodles); cut somen into 6-inch lengths and tie 5 strands together. Place 3 slices of mushroom and 1 tied somen in each bowl. Pour hot dashi over. Garnish with watercress.
• Place 3 tofu* diced, 3 precooked or raw vegetables diced, and 1 tiny sliver of cooked chicken in bowl. Pour hot dashi over.
• Place 5 name-take*, drained, in each bowl. Pour hot dashi over and garnish with a tiny carrot curl.
• Soak matsutakefu* in water just to soften. Place 1 in each bowl and pour hot dashi over. Serve immediately.
• Can always add sake—1 tablespoon per 2 cups dashi. Pass a bottle of aji oil* for guests who like theirs hot.

*see glossary

# DASHI WITH LOBSTER

5 cups dashi #2
soy sauce

3 small fresh mushrooms, each cut into 5 slices
1 small cucumber, peeled and
  cut into 15 thin slices
6 - 8 ounces cooked lobster, cut into
  25 small dice
5 small watercress sprigs
5 pieces lemon peel cut into tiny half-moon shapes

Heat dashi, season to taste with soy, bring to boil and add mushroom and cucumber slices. Boil 4 minutes. Do not overcook.
Place 3 mushroom slices, 3 cucumber slices and 5 lobster dice in each of 5 bowls.
Ladle hot dashi over and garnish with watercress and lemon peel.
Serves 5

## DASHI WITH CHICKEN BALLS

2 dried forest mushrooms, softened and
  cut into 24 small slivers
1 teaspoon soy sauce
1/2 teaspoon sake or dry sherry
1/4 teaspoon sugar

6 cups dashi #1 (see page 88)
salt
soy sauce
1 package age*, cut in halves or thirds

chicken balls (see below)
lemon peel strips
watercress sprigs

*deep fried puffy tofu

Steam mushroom slivers in soaking water, soy, sake
and sugar 10 minutes.
Bring dashi to boil and adjust seasonings to taste
with salt and soy.
In each of 8 bowls place 3 mushroom slivers, 3
chicken balls and 3 pieces of age. Ladle hot dashi
over and garnish with tiny lemon peel strips and
small watercress sprigs.
Serves 8

## CHICKEN BALLS

1/2 pound raw chicken breast, finely minced
1 egg white
1 tablespoon cornstarch
1 teaspoon salt
2 tablespoons mashed cooked peas
2 tablespoons blanched bean sprouts,
  squeezed dry and minced
1 teaspoon sake or dry sherry
1 teaspoon soy sauce

Mix ingredients, form into 24 balls, and steam
10 minutes.

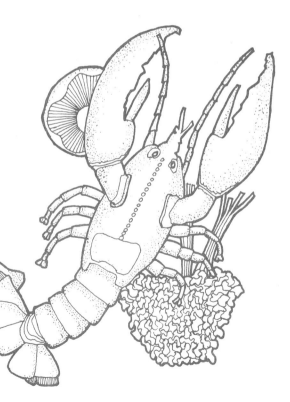

## DASHI WITH SHINGIKU

2 - 3 ounces shingiku*

6 cups dashi #2 (see page 88)
salt
soy sauce
2 eggs, beaten

18 tofu** dice
6 shrimp, cleaned, tail left on and cooked
  4 minutes in salted boiling water

raw, fresh mushroom, thinly sliced

 *chrysanthemum leaves found in Japanese markets
**see glossary

Blanch shingiku 3 minutes, drain well and chop.
Cook dashi, salt and soy to taste, and beaten egg
over low heat 6 minutes. Add shingiku and reheat.
Place 3 tofu dice and 1 shrimp in each bowl. Ladle
soup over and serve with a garnish of thinly sliced,
raw mushroom.
Serves 6

## DASHI WITH UDON

1/2 raw chicken breast, cut into 15 small
  julienne strips
1 teaspoon soy sauce
1/2 teaspoon sake or dry sherry
dash sugar

2 forest mushrooms, softened and
  cut into 15 slivers
5 water chestnuts (canned) each cut into 5 slices
1/2 cup dashi #2 (see page 88)

1/4 pound udon (thick wheat noodles)
6 cups hot water

5 cups dashi #2
soy sauce

5 tiny raw spinach leaves
5 tiny slivers of raw carrot
5 tiny strips of lemon peel

Marinate chicken strips in soy, sake and sugar
15 minutes. Combine with mushroom slivers, water
chestnut slices and dashi. Bring to boil and cook,
covered, 10 minutes. Remove cover and let liquid
boil away. Set aside and keep warm.
Cover udon with 4 cups of the hot water, bring to
boil and add rest of water. Bring back to boil, cook
1 minute, drain and rinse with cold water. Shake
colander to remove as much water as possible.
Heat dashi, adjust seasonings with soy, and reheat
with udon.
Place 3 pieces of chicken, 3 mushroom slivers and
5 slices of water chestnuts into each of 5 bowls.
Ladle dashi and udon into bowls and garnish with
spinach, carrot and lemon peel.
Serves 5

## MISOSHIRU

3 cups dashi #2  (see page 88)
1/3 cup shiromiso or akamiso*

salt
soy sauce
lemon peel
minced chives
aji oil**
 *see glossary for miso
**see glossary

Bring dashi to boil, strain miso into dashi and adjust
to taste with more miso, salt and soy sauce.
Garnish with lemon peel and minced chives. Pass
aji oil.
Serves 4

## VARIATIONS

• Add 1/2 - 1 cup tofu**, cut in 1/4-inch dice;
cook until tofu rises to surface. Do not overcook.
• Cook diced pumpkin, sliced zucchini, cubed egg-
plant or potato strips in dashi before adding miso.
Garnish with watercress.
• Add bits of bean-thread noodles**, soaked.
• See dashi variations.

**see glossary

## MISOSHIRU WITH
## CHICKEN AND VEGETABLES

7 cups dashi #2 (see· page 88)
1/4 cup each slivered raw chicken,
   carrots and pea pods
2 tablespoons chopped gobo*
1/2 cup diced potatoes

2/3 cup miso*
salt
soy sauce
shichimi pepper*

slivered green onions

*see glossary

Bring dashi to boil, add chicken and vegetables and
cook until just tender-crisp.
Add miso, heat and blend; adjust seasonings to taste
with salt, soy sauce and shichimi.
Garnish with slivered green onions.
Serves 7

## BUTAGIRU

6 cups Chinese pork stock (see page 75)
2 medium onions, cut in 8ths or 16ths
3/4 pound lean pork butt, diced
1 tablespoon soy sauce

salt

slivered green onions or watercress leaves

*Japanese pork soup for cold weather; good with pork cutlet dinner.*

Combine ingredients and cook 1 hour. Adjust seasonings with salt and garnish with slivered green onions or watercress leaves.
Serves 6

## SHRIMP BALL SOUP

3 cups dashi #1 (see page 88)
2 cups water
2 green onions, cut in 2-inch diagonal lengths
1 teaspoon soy sauce
1 recipe shrimp balls (see below)

salt

Combine dashi, water, green onions, and soy; bring to boil and add shrimp balls. Cook until balls rise to surface.
Adjust seasonings with salt.
Serves 5

## SHRIMP BALLS

1 pound raw shrimp, cleaned and finely minced
1/2 teaspoon grated fresh ginger root
2 tablespoons miso*
2 tablespoons cornstarch

*see glossary

Mix ingredients and form into small balls.

# CHAWAN MUSHI

*As delicious as it is lovely to look at!*

8 medium dried forest mushrooms, sprinkled with
  1/2 teaspoon sugar and soaked until
  soft in 1/2 cup water
12 bamboo shoot tips (canned), halved and
  cut into fan shape
8 water chestnuts (canned), cut into 3 slices each

1 tablespoon soy sauce
1/2 teaspoon sugar
1 tablespoon Mirin*

1 large chicken breast
1 teaspoon soy sauce
1/2 teaspoon salt

8 shrimp, cleaned, tail left on
1/8 teaspoon salt
2 tablespoons sake or dry sherry

8 gingko nuts
1 package kamaboko*, sliced

4 eggs
2-1/4 cups dashi #1 (see page 88)
1 tablespoon soy sauce
1 teaspoon sugar
1-1/2 teaspoons salt

8 tiny lemon peel strips
8 small watercress sprigs

*see glossary

Cut softened mushrooms into thirds; combine with soaking water, bamboo fans and water chestnuts. Cover, bring to boil and cook 10 minutes. Add soy, sugar and Mirin; cook 5 minutes, remove lid and let liquid boil away.

Cut chicken breast lengthwise and then cut with grain into 40 small strips. Combine with soy and salt.

Sprinkle shrimp with salt and drizzle sake over to coat. Let stand 10 minutes.

Place in 8 chawan bowls: 3 pieces mushroom, 3 bamboo fans, 3 slices water chestnuts, 5 strips chicken, 1 shrimp, 1 gingko nut, 1 slice kamaboko.

Beat eggs with chopsticks to blend; do not allow to foam. Add dashi and seasonings and heat slightly. Ladle into bowls, cover bowls, place in steamer and steam 15 minutes; do not allow the water to boil hard at any time. Check; custard should be set and shrimp pink.

Garnish with 1 lemon peel strip and 1 watercress sprig; put lids on and serve immediately.

Serves 8

If you don't have chawan bowls, any bowl with a lid will do. If you don't have a steamer, use 2 large kettles: place 3 pyrex bowls on bottom, top with rack and fill with water an inch above the rack. Be sure to wrap tea towels around the lids so the condensation drops do not fall into the soup. Everything can be prepared ahead of time—the surprise and delight on the faces of your guests as they view and taste is worth the effort!

# From the Americas

*Worries go down better with soup than without.*
*—Yiddish Proverb*

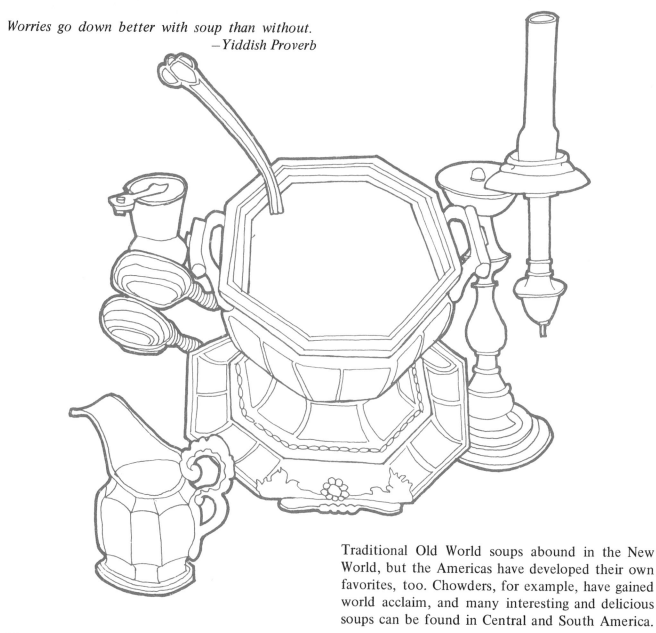

Traditional Old World soups abound in the New World, but the Americas have developed their own favorites, too. Chowders, for example, have gained world acclaim, and many interesting and delicious soups can be found in Central and South America.

94

## ALBÓNDIGAS

4 cups rich lamb stock
3 cups canned tomatoes
1/4 cup minced green pepper
1 rib celery and leaves, chopped
2 onions, sliced
6 whole cloves
1 bay leaf
1 tablespoon fresh dill
4 garlic cloves, minced
3 parsley sprigs
12 peppercorns
1/2 tablespoon salt

2 small zucchini, sliced
1/2 pound mushrooms, sliced
1 recipe lamb meatballs (see below)

dry sherry
sour cream

Bring stock, tomatoes, vegetables, herbs and seasonings to boil and simmer, covered, 2 hours. Strain. Bring stock mixture to boil, add zucchini and mushrooms; cook 10 minutes or until zucchini is tender-crisp.
Adjust seasonings, add meatballs, and heat. Serve with 1 tablespoon dry sherry in each bowl and dollops of sour cream.
Serves 6 - 8
Or season with chili powder and cinnamon to taste, or sprinkle with grated Parmesan or sharp Cheddar cheese.

## LAMB MEATBALLS

1-1/2 pounds fat-free lamb, ground
1/4 cup freshly grated Parmesan cheese
1 beaten egg
2 tablespoons milk
1/4 cup minced parsley
1/8 teaspoon rosemary
1 teaspoon black pepper
2 tablespoons lemon juice

1/4 cup ala* (optional)

*see glossary

Mix ingredients, chill, form into balls the size of large marbles and brown on all sides. If ala is used, cover and cook 10 minutes.

95

## MEXICAN CHILI SOUP

4 cups chicken stock
1/3 pound lean pork, diced
1/2 cup diced onion
1/2 cup fresh corn kernels
1 canned green chili pepper, deseeded and minced
1 cup sliced zucchini
1/2 8-ounce can tomato sauce

salt
black pepper

avocado
grated Parmesan cheese

Combine ingredients (except avocado and cheese) and simmer 30 minutes.
Adjust seasonings to taste with salt and pepper. Just before serving add avocado balls or cubes.
Pass grated Parmesan cheese.
Serves 4

## CHUPE DE CAMARONES

1 cup diced onion
2 minced garlic cloves
2 tomatoes, peeled and diced
1 - 2 teaspoons hot chili peppers, minced
1 tablespoon minced fresh oregano
1/4 cup olive oil

6 cups fish stock
1 teaspoon salt
1/2 teaspoon pepper
1/2 cup raw rice
3 medium potatoes, halved

1 cup raw fresh corn kernels
  (or 1 package frozen corn, thawed)
1-1/2 pounds medium shrimp, shelled and deveined

2 eggs beaten with
1/4 cup grated cheese*

3/4 cup evaporated milk

finely minced parsley

*The Mexican queso enchilado is best but imported Provolone may be substituted.

Sauté onion, garlic, tomatoes, peppers and oregano in oil 5 minutes, stirring to blend.
Add stock, salt and pepper; bring to boil, add rice and potato halves, and cook, covered, 30 minutes, adding corn last 10 minutes.
Raise heat to boiling, add shrimp and cook 5 minutes. Do not overcook.
Drizzle in egg and cheese mixture and boil 1 minute.
Add milk, reheat and adjust seasonings to taste. Sprinkle with finely minced parsley and serve immediately.
Serves 6 - 8

## MEXICAN TORTILLA BALL SOUP

1 tablespoon lard
6 tablespoons tomato purée
1/2 teaspoon onion juice
pinch cumin
1/4 teaspoon chili powder

8 cups beef stock
1/2 teaspoon salt
1/4 teaspoon pepper

1 recipe tortilla balls (see below)

cilantro sprigs

Melt lard in soup kettle, add tomato purée, onion juice, cumin and chili powder. Cook and stir 10 minutes over low heat to blend and improve flavors of spices. Combine with stock, season with salt and pepper, cover, bring to boil and simmer gently 10 - 15 minutes. Adjust seasonings to taste, add tortilla balls and serve with cilantro sprigs.
Serves 8 - 10
Or add 1/2 - 1 cup half-and-half cream, reheat, but do not boil.

## TORTILLA BALLS

1 pound fresh or packaged tortillas, allowed
  to get stale
1 cup milk
1 small white onion
1 garlic clove
2 ounces Parmesan or Romano cheese
1 whole egg
1 egg yolk
1/4 teaspoon salt

3 ounces lard

Soak tortillas in milk until soft. Grind with onion, garlic and cheese. Add egg, egg yolk and salt, form into balls the size of a large marble, and brown on all sides in lard.

## CHUPE HAMBURGO

1-1/2 cups minced onion
1/4 - 1/2 cup finely minced green pepper
1 garlic clove, minced
2 tablespoons butter and/or oil

1-1/2 pounds ground chuck
1/2 pound mushrooms, minced
2 cups grated carrot
2 10-1/2-ounce cans condensed cream of
  mushroom soup
1 46-ounce can vegetable or tomato juice,
  or combination
1/2 - 1 teaspoon basil
1 teaspoon salt
1/2 teaspoon paprika
1/4 teaspoon cumin
1/4 teaspoon pepper
1 1-pound can red kidney beans, drained

grated Parmesan cheese
cheese squares (see page 183)

Sauté onions, green pepper and garlic in butter and/or oil until vegetables are soft.
Raise heat, add meat and mushrooms and cook and stir with fork until meat loses its color. Add remaining ingredients (except cheeses), mix well, bring to boil, cover, and simmer gently 1/2 hour. Adjust seasonings to taste. Sprinkle with freshly grated Parmesan cheese and serve with cheese squares.
Serves 6 - 8
Or instead of tomato juice, use beef stock and fresh tomatoes, peeled, seeded and chopped. Add chunks of Velveeta cheese and heat to partially melt.

## AVOCADO GAZPACHO

1 cup sour cream
1/2 cup milk
1 cup each tomato juice and tomato sauce
2 tablespoons lemon juice
1 tablespoon olive oil
1 garlic clove, finely minced
1 bay leaf
1 cucumber, peeled, seeded and minced
1 tomato, peeled, seeded and diced
salt
black pepper
Tabasco

2 avocados
1 tablespoon lemon juice

finely minced cucumber, tomato and green pepper
garlic fingers

Beat sour cream well, then beat in milk, tomato juice, tomato sauce, lemon juice, oil and garlic. Combine well, add bay leaf, cucumber and tomato. Season with salt, pepper and Tabasco and chill thoroughly to blend flavors.
Remove bay leaf. Mash the avocados with lemon juice and blend into tomato mixture just before serving. Adjust seasonings and serve in chilled bowls. Garnish with finely minced cucumber, tomato and green pepper, and serve with garlic fingers.
Serves 3 - 4

## SPICY GUACAMOLE WITH SHRIMP

1 large avocado, peeled and diced
1 cup buttermilk
1/2 cup yoghurt
1 tablespoon mayonnaise
1 tablespoon minced green onion
2-1/2 tablespoons lemon juice
1 tomato, peeled and diced
1 - 2 canned green chilis, deseeded and minced
1/8 teaspoon each cumin and coriander

bay or canned shrimp
fresh coriander

Purée ingredients (except shrimp and coriander) in blender and chill. Adjust seasonings and serve in chilled bowls; garnish with chilled bay or canned shrimp and fresh coriander.
Serves 3 - 4
Serve with tortilla chips.

## SWEET POTATO SOUP

1 tablespoon bacon fat
1 cup chopped onion
3 ribs celery, chopped
1 pound sweet potatoes, peeled and sliced
5 cups chicken stock
1/2 teaspoon salt
1/4 teaspoon black pepper
nutmeg

sour cream

Sauté onion, celery and sweet potatoes in bacon fat 5 minutes. Add stock, cover, bring to boil and simmer until soft.
Purée in blender and reheat. Season to taste with salt, pepper and nutmeg. Pass a bowl of sour cream.
Serves 6

## GUMBO

2 tablespoons bacon fat
1/4 cup minced onion
1/4 cup minced celery
2 tablespoons minced green pepper

1 teaspoon freshly grated lemon peel
1 bay leaf
3 tablespoons minced parsley
3 tomatoes, peeled and diced or
2 cups canned tomatoes, broken up
1 minced garlic clove
1/2 teaspoon black pepper
1/2 teaspoon salt
1/4 teaspoon cumin
6 cups chicken stock
1 cup fresh corn kernels
1 package frozen okra, sliced

leftover chicken bits
leftover ham bits
sausages, sliced and cooked

1/2 teaspoon filé powder*

crisp bacon bits

*see glossary

Brown onion, celery and green pepper in bacon fat. Combine with lemon peel, bay leaf, parsley, tomatoes, garlic, seasonings and stock. Cover, bring to boil and cook 10 minutes.
Add corn and okra and cook over high heat 8 minutes, stirring occasionally. Add chicken, ham and sausage.
Remove bay leaf, reheat and adjust seasonings to taste. Add filé powder just before serving. Sprinkle with crisp bacon bits.
Serves 6 - 8

## CREAM OF SCALLOP SOUP

1 pound Eastern scallops, cut in 1/2-inch pieces
juice of 1 or 2 limes
2 8-ounce bottles clam juice or
  2 cups liquid from steamed clams
1 tablespoon butter
1/4 cup chopped green pepper (optional)
2 green onions and tops, sliced
1/4 teaspoon each Worcestershire sauce, garlic
  powder and dry mustard

2 egg yolks, beaten
1 cup half-and-half cream

paprika
minced parsley, chives and green onions

Marinate scallops in lime juice several hours. Drain and dry with paper toweling.

Sauté green pepper and green onions in butter 3 minutes, add clam juice and seasonings, bring to boil, add scallops and simmer 4 - 5 minutes until scallops are just done. Be careful—overcooking toughens them.

Beat yolks with cream, add 1/2 cup hot soup and return to rest of soup. Reheat but do not boil.

Adjust seasonings to taste, sprinkle with lots of paprika and minced parsley, chives and green onions. Serve with pumpernickel toast.

Serves 3 - 4

Or reduce clam juice measurement to 1-1/2 cups, add 1 7-1/2-ounce can minced clams, and add 1 cup cooked potato dice. Garnish with chopped tomatoes.

## GARLIC SOUP

20 - 25 garlic cloves, peeled
1/4 cup olive oil

8 cups chicken stock
1 tablespoon chicken stock base
1 teaspoon soy sauce
1/4 teaspoon each sage and black pepper
2 whole cloves
1/2 teaspoon each oregano, thyme and paprika
8 parsley sprigs

1/2 cup dry sherry

8 toasted sour dough French bread slices
8 tablespoons each grated Gruyère and Parmesan
  cheese

Sauté garlic in oil until just starting to turn golden. Add stock, stock base, seasonings and herbs. Cover, bring to boil and simmer 1 hour.

Strain, reheat and adjust seasonings. Just before serving add sherry.

Ladle soup into heated ovenproof bowls, top with toast, sprinkle with 1 tablespoon of each cheese, and broil to melt cheese.

Serves 8

Or omit cheese. Top each piece of toast with a small raw egg. Ladle hot soup over to poach egg and garnish with coriander.

## CREAMY LOBSTER WITH CHEESE

1 8-ounce lobster tail, cooked and minced
1/4 cup dry sherry

2 tablespoons butter
3 tablespoons finely minced onion
1 teaspoon finely minced shallots
2 tablespoons finely minced celery

1-1/2 tablespoons flour
2 cups half-and-half cream

2 tablespoons finely minced parsley

1/2 teaspoon salt
1/4 teaspoon Lemon Garlic*
1/4 teaspoon white pepper

milk

1/4 cup grated imported Provolone cheese

paprika
minced Chinese chives*

*see glossary

Soak lobster in sherry at least 1 hour.

Steam onion, shallots, and celery in butter, covered, 10 minutes.

Sprinkle with flour, cook and stir 3 minutes and gradually add cream. Cook and stir until smooth and slightly thickened.

Add lobster and sherry, and parsley. Reheat and season with salt, Lemon Garlic and pepper. Adjust to taste.

Just before serving add cheese and heat to melt. Thin with milk if desired.

Dust with paprika and sprinkle with minced Chinese chives.

Serves 3 - 4

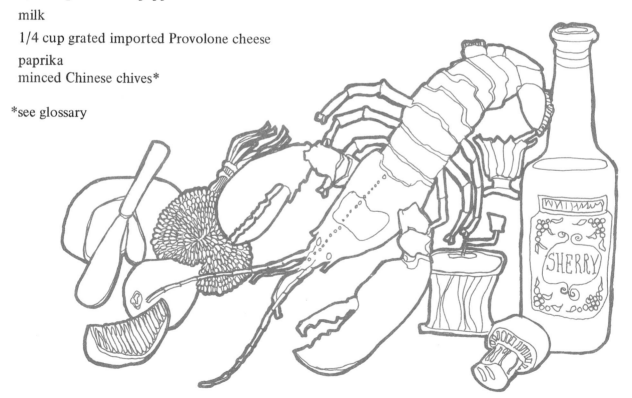

## CREAMY CLAM WITH SPINACH

3 tablespoons minced onion
2 tablespoons butter
1 tablespoon minced shallots
1 minced garlic clove

2 packages frozen chopped spinach, thawed
1/4 teaspoon black pepper
1/2 teaspoon seafood seasoning

2 7-1/2-ounce cans minced clams and juice

1 - 2 tablespoons lemon juice
2 cups half-and-half cream

grated Parmesan cheese

Sauté onions in butter until soft. Add shallots and garlic, and cook 3 minutes. Add spinach, pepper and seafood seasoning; cover and cook until spinach is tender.
Purée half of spinach mixture in blender with 1 can clams. Remove to saucepan and repeat with remaining clams and spinach.
Combine spinach and clams with lemon juice and cream; reheat but do not boil. Adjust seasonings to taste and serve with a sprinkling of freshly grated Parmesan cheese.
Serves 4
Or season with nutmeg. Serve very cold in chilled bowls, garnished with hard-cooked egg slices, lemon slices and minced parsley.

## CREAM OF CLAM BROTH

2-2/3 cups fresh clam juice or 3 7-ounce bottles
1 cup water
1 tablespoon chicken stock base
1-1/2 cups half-and-half cream

3 tablespoons minced shallots
2 tablespoons butter
2 tablespoons flour

Tabasco
white pepper
salt

1/3 cup dry white wine
butter bits

paprika
finely minced green onion tops

Combine clam juice, water, stock base and cream; heat without boiling.
Sauté shallots in butter until soft, sprinkle with flour and stir and cook 3 minutes. Gradually add clam mixture; stir and cook until smooth and slightly thickened.
Season with Tabasco, pepper and salt, and adjust to taste.
Just before serving add wine, swirl in butter bits and sprinkle with paprika and finely minced green onion tops.
Serves 6
Or ladle into ovenproof bowls, top with whipped cream and broil to brown. Sprinkle with minced chives.

## CRAB WITH PASTA

1 pound flaked crabmeat
1/4 cup dry sherry

1 cup minced celery
3/4 cup minced onion
1/2 cup minced green pepper
3 tablespoons butter

1 teaspoon flour
1/2 teaspoon sugar
1 teaspoon chili powder

2 cups half-and-half cream or milk

1/4 cup small seashell pasta, cooked *al dente* in
  salted boiling water

1/2 teaspoon salt
1/4 teaspoon white pepper
1/2 teaspoon Worcestershire sauce

whipped cream
minced parsley

*Very rich—quite thick!*

Combine crab and sherry and marinate at least
1 hour.
Sauté celery, onion, and green pepper in butter
until vegetables are tender.
Sprinkle with flour, sugar and chili; cook and stir
3 minutes.
Gradually add cream or milk; cook and stir until
smooth and slightly thickened.
Add crab, sherry and pasta. Reheat without boiling
and season with salt, pepper and Worcestershire
sauce. Adjust to taste.
Garnish with whipped cream dollops and minced
parsley. Pass the peppermill.
Serves 4

## BONGO-BONGO

8 ounces fresh oysters and liquid
1/2 cup chopped frozen spinach, cooked
  and well drained
1 tablespoon butter
1/4 cup minced mushrooms
1/2 tablespoon flour

1 cup milk

1-1/2 cups half-and-half cream
1/4 teaspoon garlic powder
1 teaspoon Worcestershire sauce
1/2 teaspoon each thyme, salt and black pepper

lemon slices

Sauté mushrooms in butter until soft, sprinkle with
flour and cook and stir 3 minutes. Gradually add
milk; cook and stir until smooth and slightly thickened. Purée in blender with oysters and spinach.
Reheat with seasonings and cream; adjust to taste.
Cool, chill and serve in chilled bowls with lemon
slices.
Serves 4 - 6
To serve hot, heat with 2 tablespoons butter and
garnish with heavy cream whipped with soy sauce.

## POACHED FISH IN BROTH

6 cups basic fish stock fortified with white wine,
  tarragon and lemon juice

3 haddock filets (or other firm fish)
aioli sauce (see page 180)
anchovy-egg sauce (see below)

lemon wedges
minced parsley

Bring stock to boil and adjust seasonings to taste.
Lower heat and gently poach fish 10 minutes or
until tender. Do not overcook.
Place half a filet in each soup bowl and top with a
tablespoon of sauce.
Garnish with lemon wedges and sprinkle with parsley.
Serves 6
Or cut down on proportions and serve as a soup
appetizer.
If thicker soup is desired, bind with a liaison of 2
egg yolks beaten into 1/2 cup hot soup and
returned to rest of soup.

## ANCHOVY-EGG SAUCE

3 hard-cooked eggs, sieved
1-1/2 teaspoons cream
1 - 1-1/2 teaspoons anchovy paste
2 drops Tabasco
1/2 - 3/4 teaspoon Worcestershire sauce
3 - 4 tablespoons mayonnaise

Mix ingredients and adjust seasonings to taste.

# COLD SHRIMP BISQUE

1-1/2 pounds raw shrimp, cleaned and deveined
lemon juice

2 cups milk
1 cup half-and-half cream
1/4 cup each minced onion and celery
1/2 - 1 teaspoon anchovy paste
bouquet garni of:
  1 sprig thyme
  3 sprigs parsley
  6 peppercorns
  1 small bay leaf
1-1/2 tablespoons raw rice

1 cup heavy cream

Tabasco
salt
white pepper
Worcestershire sauce

pimiento strips

Cook 1/2 pound of the shrimp in rapidly boiling salted water with lots of lemon juice 4 - 5 minutes until pink; do not overcook. Dice and reserve.

Combine rest of shrimp, cream, onion, celery, anchovy paste, bouquet garni and rice. Cover, bring to gentle boil, and simmer 45 minutes, stirring occasionally.

Discard bouquet garni, and purée bisque in blender. Add cream and chill. Adjust seasonings with Tabasco, salt, pepper and Worcestershire sauce and serve in chilled bowls. Garnish with reserved shrimp and pimiento strips.

Serves 4 - 6

Or sprinkle with minced fresh dill.

# HOT SHRIMP BISQUE

2 pounds raw shrimp, cleaned and deveined

3 tablespoons butter
2 tablespoons each minced carrot, onion
  and celery
1 minced garlic clove

1 bay leaf
1/2 teaspoon thyme
3 tablespoons minced parsley
1 tablespoon lemon juice
2 cups chicken stock
1 cup fish stock

1 cup half-and-half cream
1/2 cup heavy cream
salt
white pepper
Tabasco
Worcestershire sauce
1/2 cup dry white wine

minced dill

Mince 1-1/2 pounds of the shrimp and set aside.
Melt butter until bubbly and over high heat sauté the rest of the shrimp with carrot, onion, celery and garlic 5 - 8 minutes, stirring constantly. Do not overcook. Remove shrimp, dice and reserve.
Combine minced raw shrimp, bay leaf, thyme, parsley, lemon juice and stocks. Cover, bring to boil and simmer 45 minutes, stirring occasionally.
Discard bay leaf. Purée mixture in blender and reheat with creams and reserved shrimp. Adjust seasonings to taste with salt, pepper, Tabasco and Worcestershire sauce.
Just before serving add wine. Serve with a generous sprinkling of minced dill.
Serves 4 - 6

# COLD BUTTERMILK-SHRIMP BISQUE

1-1/2 pounds raw shrimp, cleaned and deveined
3 cups water
1 tablespoon salt
1/4 cup lemon juice

3 cups buttermilk
1 cucumber, peeled, seeded and grated
2 tablespoons Dijon-style mustard
1/2 teaspoon horseradish
1/4 teaspoon each sugar and garlic powder
1/2 teaspoon salt
1/2 teaspoon Lemon Dill*
1 tablespoon finely minced celery

2 tablespoons minced chives

minced parsley

*see glossary

Bring water, salt and lemon juice to rolling boil, add shrimp and boil 4 - 5 minutes until pink. Do not overcook. Drain and plunge into ice water. Cut 1/2 cup of shrimp into 1/2-inch dice and reserve. Coarsely chop remainder and purée in blender with 1 cup of the buttermilk.
Combine with rest of buttermilk, cucumber, seasonings and celery.
Chill and adjust seasonings to taste.
Stir in chives, serve in chilled bowls and top with reserved shrimp dice and minced parsley.
Serves 6

## CLAM & LEEK BISQUE

2 cups minced leeks, white and some green
1/4 cup each minced celery and onion
2 cloves minced garlic
3 tablespoons minced carrot
4 tablespoons butter and/or rendered chicken fat

4 cups rich beef stock
1-1/2 cups diced potatoes

1 7-1/2-ounce can minced clams and liquid
1 7-1/2-ounce can chopped clams and liquid
1 cup half-and-half cream

salt
white pepper
black pepper
Lemon Celery*
butter bits

finely minced parsley and garlic
paprika

*see glossary

Sauté leeks, celery, onion, garlic and carrot in butter and/or fat until leeks are soft.
Add stock and potatoes, cover, bring to a boil and simmer until potatoes are tender. Purée in blender.
Combine potato mixture with clams and add cream.
Reheat, but do not boil. Season to taste with salt, white and black pepper and Lemon Celery. Stir in butter bits.
Sprinkle with lots of finely minced parsley, finely minced garlic, and paprika.
Serves 6 - 8
For richer bisque, add heavy cream.

# ABALONE CHOWDER

3/4 cup minced green onions, leeks and/or onions
1 minced garlic clove
1/4 pound diced salt pork
3 tablespoons butter

2 cups chicken stock
1 cup fish stock or clam juice
1-1/2 cups diced baking potatoes
1/4 teaspoon Lemon Celery*
1/4 teaspoon black pepper

1 1-pound can abalone, drained and minced
1-1/2 cups half-and-half cream
1/2 cup heavy cream
1/2 teaspoon anchovy paste

salt
butter bits
paprika

*see glossary

Sauté onions, garlic and salt pork in butter until onions are soft.
Add stocks, potatoes and seasonings; cover, bring to boil and simmer 10 minutes. Potatoes should stay crisp.
Add abalone, creams and anchovy paste. Blend well and reheat without boiling.
Adjust seasonings with salt, swirl in butter bits and sprinkle with paprika.
Serves 6

# CRAB CHOWDER

4 slices bacon, diced
2 tablespoons flour
3 cups milk, or half milk and half light cream
1 tablespoon onion juice
1 cup tomato juice
1/4 teaspoon each basil, marjoram, garlic powder and black pepper

1 cup cooked diced potatoes
2 cups flaked crab meat

salt
or celery salt

paprika
reserved bacon bits

Sauté bacon until crisp, remove with slotted spoon and reserve. Pour off all but 1-1/2 tablespoons of fat.
Sprinkle with flour and cook and stir 3 minutes. Gradually add milk and/or cream; cook and stir until smooth and slightly thickened.
Add onion juice, tomato juice and seasonings; simmer, covered, 10 minutes.
Add potatoes and crab, reheat and adjust seasonings to taste with salt or celery salt.
Sprinkle with paprika and reserved bacon bits.
Serves 4
Or garnish with crab legs and lemon wedges.

## TROUT CHOWDER

5 large trout
2 cups water
bouquet garni of
  2 parsley sprigs
  1 bay leaf
  1/2 cup celery leaves
  1 sprig thyme
  1/2 medium onion stuck with
  2 cloves

1/2 cup diced onions
1/2 cup diced celery
1/4 cup diced carrot
3 tablespoons butter
1 - 1-1/2 cups diced potato
2 cups milk
1/2 cup heavy cream

salt
white or black pepper
garlic powder
celery seed

Cook trout in water with bouquet garni until it flakes when tested with a fork. Remove and set aside to cool. Discard bouquet garni, add vegetables, cover, bring to boil and simmer 5 minutes. Add butter and potatoes and cook until potatoes are just tender-crisp.

Add milk and reheat. While vegetables are cooking, remove meat from trout to make about 2-1/2 cups. Add to hot chowder with heavy cream; reheat but do not boil.

Season and adjust to taste. Serve with French bread and sweet butter.

Serves 6 - 8

## CLAM CHOWDER

1 cup minced green onions, leeks and/or onion
1 minced garlic clove
1/4 pound diced salt pork
3 tablespoons butter

3 cups rich chicken stock
2-1/2 cups diced baking potatoes
1 bay leaf
1/4 teaspoon thyme
1/8 teaspoon allspice
1/4 teaspoon black pepper
3 dozen clams, shucked, and their juices*
1 cup bottled clam juice

1-1/2 cups half-and-half cream
1/2 cup heavy cream

salt
butter bits

paprika
slivered green onions

*Substitute 3 7-1/2-ounce cans minced clams and their juice for fresh clams and bottled juice.

Sauté onions, garlic and salt pork in butter until onions are soft.
Add stock, potatoes, bay leaf, thyme, allspice and pepper. Cover, bring to boil and simmer 10 minutes. Potatoes should remain crisp. Remove bay leaf.
Mince clams, add to soup with juices and creams, and reheat without boiling.
Season with salt and adjust to taste.
Stir in butter bits and sprinkle with paprika and slivered green onions.
Serves 6
For garlic lovers, finely minced raw garlic sprinkled on top of soup just before serving adds a real zest.

# CORN CHOWDER

2 cups fresh raw corn kernels
  from 4 - 5 ears of corn*
3 cups chicken stock
1/2 teaspoon sugar
1/2 teaspoon salt
1/2 cup minced onion
1/4 cup minced celery
1/4 cup butter
1/2 teaspoon dry mustard
1/2 teaspoon sugar
1/4 teaspoon black pepper
1 tablespoon lemon juice
1-1/2 cups diced potatoes (optional)

2 cups half-and-half cream
3 drops Tabasco
1/2 teaspoon Worcestershire sauce

1 egg yolk, beaten
3/4 cup heavy cream

3/4 teaspoon salt
1/4 teaspoon thyme

paprika
minced parsley

*Defrosted frozen corn may be used, but the flavor
is not the same.

Cut kernels from corn, scraping as much pulp and milk off as possible. Boil cobs in stock with sugar and salt 15 minutes. Strain and reserve stock.
Sauté kernels, onion and celery in butter with mustard, sugar and pepper until onions are soft but not browned.
Add lemon juice, reserved stock and potatoes, if used. Cover, bring to boil and simmer 15 minutes. Add cream, Tabasco and Worcestershire sauce. Reheat. Beat yolk and heavy cream, whisk in 1/2 cup hot soup and return to rest of soup. Heat but do not boil.
Season with salt and thyme and adjust to taste.
Serve sprinkled with paprika and minced parsley.
Serves 6
Watercress and heated French-fried onions also make a good garnish.

# Other Ports of Call

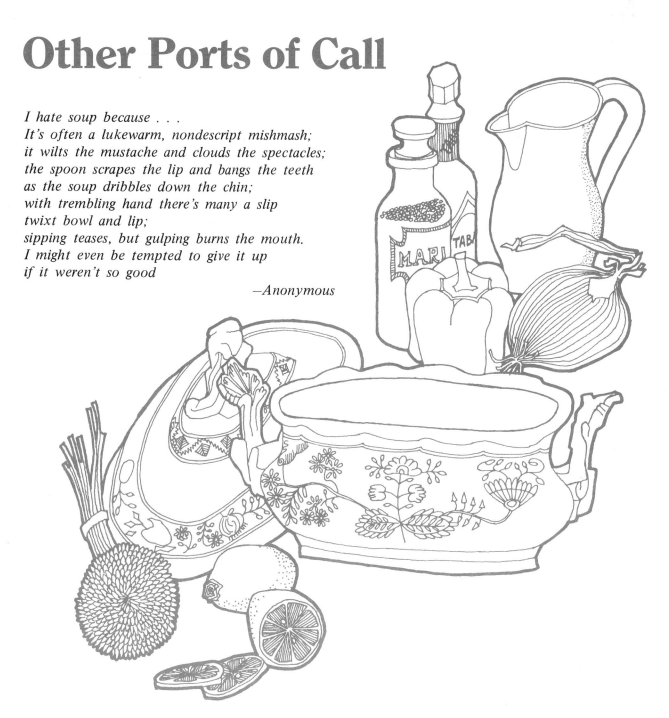

*I hate soup because . . .*
*It's often a lukewarm, nondescript mishmash;*
*it wilts the mustache and clouds the spectacles;*
*the spoon scrapes the lip and bangs the teeth*
*as the soup dribbles down the chin;*
*with trembling hand there's many a slip*
*twixt bowl and lip;*
*sipping teases, but gulping burns the mouth.*
*I might even be tempted to give it up*
*if it weren't so good*

*—Anonymous*

## CHEESE AND ONION SOUP

1-1/2 cups minced onion
1/4 cup butter
3 tablespoons flour
1/2 teaspoon seasoned salt
1/8 teaspoon cayenne pepper
1/4 teaspoon black pepper
1/2 teaspoon paprika
1/4 teaspoon sage
3 cups milk
1 cup half-and-half cream
2 cups grated sharp Cheddar cheese
1/2 teaspoon Worcestershire sauce
3 drops Tabasco
3 tablespoons minced parsley

whipped cream
minced chives

*This is a very rich soup!*

Sauté onion in butter until soft. Add flour and seasonings, cook and stir 3 minutes and gradually add milk and cream. Cook and stir until smooth and thickened. Add cheese and stir until melted. Season with Worcestershire, Tabasco and parsley, and adjust to taste.
Garnish with dollops of whipped cream and sprinkle with minced chives.
Serves 6
Or for milder flavor, substitute Monterey Jack cheese.

## CREAMY BELL PEPPER

1 cup diced green pepper
1/2 cup diced onion
1 minced garlic clove
2 tablespoons butter

2 tablespoons flour
1/2 teaspoon marjoram
3 cups chicken stock

1-1/2 cups milk and/or half-and-half cream

1/4 teaspoon white pepper
1/4 teaspoon Lemon Chef*

salt

raw green pepper, sliced paper thin
lemon slices

*see glossary

Sauté green pepper, onion and garlic in butter until soft.
Sprinkle with flour and marjoram; cook and stir 3 minutes. Gradually add stock, cook and stir until smooth and slightly thickened, cover and simmer gently 30 minutes.
Purée in blender, add milk and/or cream and season with pepper and Lemon Chef. Reheat and adjust seasonings with salt; or chill and adjust seasonings.
Garnish with green pepper slices and/or lemon slices.
Serves 4 - 6

## BLACK OLIVE SOUP

4 cups rich chicken stock
1-1/2 cups pitted ripe olives, sliced
3 tablespoons grated onion
2 garlic cloves

2 eggs, beaten
1 cup half-and-half cream
1 teaspoon Worcestershire sauce
1/2 teaspoon Lemon Celery*
1/4 cup juice from olives

salt — be careful!
Tabasco

paprika
grated onion

*see glossary

Simmer olives, onion and garlic in stock, covered, for 20 minutes. Discard garlic.
Beat eggs into cream, whisk in 1/2 cup hot stock, and return to rest of soup. Season with Worcestershire sauce, Lemon Celery and juice. Adjust to taste with salt and Tabasco, reheat and serve with a sprinkle of paprika and more grated onion.
Serves 4
Or cool, chill and serve in chilled bowls with minced parsley.

## DANISH PORT SALUT

2 tablespoons butter
1 cup diced kohlrabi or young turnips
1/4 cup each minced onion and
   white part of leeks
2 cups diced potatoes
3 cups chicken stock
2 cups milk
1 can (15-1/2-ounces) *small* red beans,
   not kidney beans (Hunt's)

1 cup heavy cream
2 cups grated Danish Port Salut cheese
salt
white pepper

butter bits
minced green onions
minced parsley

Sauté kohlrabi or turnips, onions and leeks in butter until soft but not browned. Add potatoes, stock, milk and beans; cover, bring to boil and simmer gently 45 minutes. (Will look curdled, but it doesn't matter.)
Add cream and 1-1/2 cups of the cheese; cook and stir to melt cheese and reheat; do not boil. Season to taste with salt and white pepper, stir in butter bits and serve with green onions, parsley and remaining cheese on top.
Serves 6 - 8

## BONE MARROW WITH VEGETABLES

3 pounds beef marrow bones, sawed into
  3-inch pieces*
1-1/2 cups chopped onion
4 minced garlic cloves
6 cups water
1 teaspoon salt
1/2 teaspoon black pepper

1/2 cup thinly sliced carrots
1/2 cup thinly sliced onion
1 cup celery, sliced thinly on diagonal

3 tomatoes, peeled and diced

1 cup barley cooked 1-1/2 hours in
  salted water and drained

beef stock

minced fresh herbs

*If you want to keep the marrow intact, wrap each
  bone in cheesecloth and tie securely.

*This soup has an unusual, delicate flavor. The recipe
seems complicated only because of the necessity to
remove the fat from the marrow gradually.*

Combine bones, onion, garlic, water, salt and pep-
per. Cover, bring to boil and simmer 1-1/2 hours.
Skim off any scum that rises to surface.
Cool, chill and defat. Reheat and continue cooking
1-1/2 hours, skimming surface as needed.
Cool, chill and defat. Remove bones and marrow.
Cut up as much marrow as desired and reserve.
Strain soup, bring to boil and add carrots, onion
and celery. Cook 10 minutes and add tomatoes.
Cook 2 more minutes, add barley and reserved
marrow and heat. Adjust seasonings to taste and
add stock if barley has made the soup too thick.
Sprinkle with minced fresh herbs and serve with
cheese fingers.
Serves 6
Or can season with mace and powdered cloves to
taste.

115

## PEANUT BUTTER SOUP

2 tablespoons butter
2 tablespoons flour
4 cups milk

3/4 cup chopped onion
2 tablespoons grated Parmesan cheese
1/4 teaspoon celery seed
1/2 teaspoon salt
1/4 teaspoon black pepper
1 crumbled bay leaf
1/3 cup peanut butter

macaroons (see below)

crisp bacon bits or
chopped peanuts

Melt butter until bubbly, sprinkle with flour and cook and stir 3 minutes. Gradually add milk; cook and stir until smooth and slightly thickened.
Add onion, cheese, seasonings, bay leaf and peanut butter. Cover, bring to boil and simmer 15 minutes. Strain, adjust seasonings and ladle hot soup over macaroons in 4 - 6 bowls. Sprinkle with bacon bits or peanuts. Macaroons should stay crisp.
Serves 4 - 6
Or omit the macaroons, chill and serve in chilled bowls; sprinkle with chopped peanuts.

### MACAROONS

2 tablespoons softened butter
1/2 cup grated almonds
1/2 cup grated stale bread
1 tablespoon sugar
1 egg, beaten

Combine ingredients and drop by teaspoonfuls into hot fat. Cook until golden and crisp, drain on paper toweling and serve immediately.

## CREAMY TAPIOCA SOUP

1 cup half-and-half cream
1/4 cup chopped leeks
1/3 cup chopped onion
1 minced garlic clove

5 cups rich chicken stock
1/3 cup minute tapioca

1 egg yolk, beaten

1/8 teaspoon mace
1/4 teaspoon white pepper
1/2 teaspoon salt

6 teaspoons butter bits
minced chervil

Bring cream, leeks, onion and garlic just to boil and simmer 15 minutes. Strain and cool.

Bring stock to boil, gradually add tapioca, stirring constantly, and lower heat. Cover and cook 10 minutes.

Beat egg yolk and cooled cream, whisk in 1/2 cup hot soup and return to rest of soup. Reheat without boiling.

Season with mace, pepper and salt, adjusting to taste. Swirl in butter bits and sprinkle with minced chervil.

Serves 6

Or omit butter bits. Just before serving add 1/4 cup dry sherry.

*Garlic lovers: Here is an unusual flavor!*

## GARLIC SOUP WITH POTATO BALLS

6 medium potatoes, quartered
3/4 cup chopped onion
1/2 teaspoon salt

5 pressed garlic cloves (or more!)
1/2 teaspoon salt
2 egg yolks, beaten
1 cup olive oil

salt
black pepper
3 tablespoons flour

minced parsley or
minced cilantro

Boil potatoes and onion in salted water until soft. Drain, reserving liquid, and force potatoes through food mill or sieve.

Blend garlic, salt and egg yolks; gradually add oil, stirring constantly. Combine with sieved potato and reserve 3/4 cup. Add remaining garlic-potato mixture to reserved potato water and blend well. Adjust seasonings with salt and pepper.

Mix reserved potato-garlic mixture with flour, adding more flour if needed to form small balls.

Return soup to boil, add balls, lower heat slightly and cook 5 minutes.

Garnish with minced parsley or cilantro.

Serves 6

Or season with a little vinegar.

# CHEDDAR CHEESE VELOUTÉ

4 cups rich chicken stock
2 leeks, white only, chopped
1/2 cup chopped onion
1/3 cup chopped celery
6 parsley sprigs
1/2 teaspoon turmeric

3 tablespoons cornstarch mixed with
3 tablespoons cold water
1-1/2 cups grated sharp Cheddar cheese
1/4 teaspoon each white pepper, paprika,
  and nutmeg

2 egg yolks, beaten
1-1/2 cups half-and-half cream
1/3 cup dry white wine

chili powder
salt

minced chives
paprika

Bring stock, vegetables, parsley and turmeric to boil, cover and simmer 1 hour. Cool and strain.
Reheat, add cornstarch-water binder, and cook and stir until smooth and slightly thickened.
Add cheese and seasonings and heat gently to melt cheese.
Beat yolks into cream, whisk in 1/2 cup hot soup, and return to rest of soup. Reheat. Do not boil.
Add wine and adjust seasonings to taste with chili powder and salt.
Sprinkle with minced chives and paprika and serve with mushroom cornucopias.
Serves 6
Or garnish with generous amount of grated carrot.

# MUSTARD SOUP

2 tablespoons each butter and flour
2-1/2 cups chicken stock
1-1/4 cups milk
1/2 teaspoon salt
1/4 teaspoon white pepper
1-1/2 teaspoons onion juice

2 egg yolks, beaten
3 tablespoons prepared mustard
3 tablespoons cream

whipped cream
minced parsley

Melt butter until bubbly, sprinkle with flour, cook and stir 3 minutes. Gradually add stock and milk; cook and stir until smooth and slightly thickened. Season with salt, pepper and onion juice.
Combine yolks, mustard and cream. Whisk in 1/2 cup hot soup and return to rest of soup. Reheat; do not boil. Adjust seasonings to taste.
Garnish with whipped cream dollops and minced parsley.
Serves 4
Or add 1/2 cup heavy cream, chill, and serve in chilled bowls.

## GAME BROTH WITH FORCEMEAT BALLS

6 cups stock made from any game

1 recipe forcemeat balls made from
 game used (see page 179)

3/4 cup heavy cream
1 egg yolk, beaten

minced chervil
garlic croutons

Heat stock; beat cream and yolk and whisk in 1/2 cup hot stock. Return to rest of stock, reheat without boiling and add forcemeat balls cooked separately in salted water.

Garnish with minced chervil and serve with garlic croutons.

Serves 6

Or omit the liaison of cream and egg; add 1/2 cup dry red wine and 1 tablespoon red currant jelly. Reheat.

## PEANUT SOUP

2 teaspoons grated onion
1/2 cup peanuts, ground
3 tablespoons butter
3 tablespoons flour
3-1/2 cups rich chicken stock

1 egg yolk, beaten
1 cup heavy cream

Tabasco
celery salt
white pepper
lemon juice

lemon slices
toasted peanuts

Sauté onion and peanuts in butter 5 minutes, stirring constantly. Sprinkle with flour, cook and stir 3 minutes, and gradually add stock. Cook and stir until smooth and slightly thickened; cover and simmer gently 15 - 20 minutes.

Combine yolk and cream, whisk in 1/2 cup hot soup, and return to rest of soup.

Season to taste with Tabasco, celery salt, white pepper and lemon juice; thin with more stock if desired. Reheat but do not boil.

Serve with lemon slices and extra toasted peanuts.

Serves 4 - 6

Or add 2 tablespoons each of finely minced hot red pepper and green pepper the last few minutes of cooking.

## RAHM-SUPPE MIT NOCKERL

3 tablespoons butter
3 tablespoons flour

3 cups chicken or veal stock
3 cups milk

1 large onion, halved and stuck with 4 cloves
6 parsley sprigs
1 thyme sprig
1/2 teaspoon cumin
1/4 teaspoon nutmeg
4 peppercorns

1 cup sour cream

1 package Nockerl-Griess*

minced parsley

*Nockerl-Griess is a semolina dumpling mixture available at health-food stores.

Melt butter until bubbly, sprinkle with flour, cook and stir 3 minutes.

Gradually add stock and milk; cook and stir until smooth and slightly thickened.

Add onion, herbs and seasonings. Cover, bring to gentle boil and simmer 1-1/2 hours. Strain.

Beat 1/2 cup hot soup with sour cream and return to rest of soup. Reheat; do not boil. Adjust seasonings to taste.

Just before serving add Nockerl cooked in salted water according to package directions. Sprinkle with minced parsley.

Serves 6

## MANDELSUPPE

3/4 cup blanched almonds

1 tablespoon minced onion
2 tablespoons butter
2 tablespoons flour
2 cups chicken stock

1 cup evaporated milk

1/2 teaspoon salt
1/8 teaspoon white pepper
almond extract or
rose water

Grind almonds in blender.
Sauté onion in butter until butter bubbles. Sprinkle with flour, cook and stir 3 minutes and gradually add stock. Cook and stir until smooth and slightly thickened.
Add milk and almonds; cover and simmer 30 minutes.
Adjust seasonings to taste with salt, pepper and almond extract (be careful!) or rosewater.
Serves 4
The consistency of this soup is gritty; if smoothness is preferred, simmer almonds in 1 cup stock, covered, for several hours to extract flavor. Force through sieve and add to rest of soup.

## BIERSUPPE

4 teaspoons butter
1-1/2 tablespoons flour
2 tablespoons extra-fine sugar

1 quart light beer or malt liquor
2 tablespoons lemon juice
1/2 teaspoon freshly grated lemon peel
1/8 teaspoon cinnamon

2 eggs, separated

cinnamon
tiny lemon peel strips

Melt butter until bubbly, sprinkle with flour and sugar, cook and stir until caramel colored.
Gradually add beer, cook and stir until smooth and slightly thickened. Add lemon juice, peel and cinnamon.
Beat egg yolks and whisk in 1/2 cup hot soup; return to rest of soup and reheat without boiling.
Whip egg whites and float on top with a dusting of cinnamon and lemon peel strips.
Serves 6

## CZECH CABBAGE SOUP

4 cups chicken stock
2 cups shredded cabbage
1 teaspoon caraway seeds
1-1/2 teaspoons instant onion

1 cup milk or half-and-half cream

salt
pepper
caraway seeds
1/4 pound thin noodles, cooked

Combine stock, cabbage, caraway and onion, cover, bring to boil and simmer until cabbage is soft.
Purée in blender, reheat with cream or milk or combination, season to taste with salt and pepper and more caraway seeds. Add noodles, reheat and serve.
Serves 4 - 6

## OTTO'S GRAPENUTS SOUP

6 cups rich beef stock
4 onions, thinly sliced

1-1/2 cups Grapenuts cereal
6 tablespoons grated Parmesan cheese
pinch nutmeg
2 tablespoons butter, melted

Cook onions in stock until tender.
Combine grapenuts, cheese and nutmeg; place in bottom of soup tureen.
Pour butter over and then the stock and onions.
Serve immediately—the grapenuts should stay crisp!
Serves 6

## KULAJDA (CZECH)

3/4 pound mushrooms, thinly sliced
2 tablespoons each butter and olive oil
1/2 teaspoon each garlic powder, white
  pepper and oregano
1/4 teaspoon salt
dash cayenne pepper
1 teaspoon caraway seeds (optional)
2 teaspoons lemon juice

1-1/2 tablespoons flour
1 teaspoon paprika
3 tablespoons minced parsley
3 cups stock

1 cup sour cream
2 - 3 egg yolks, beaten

minced fresh dill or
caraway seeds
paprika

Sauté mushrooms in butter and oil, seasoning while they are cooking with garlic powder, pepper, oregano, salt, cayenne, caraway and lemon juice, until mushrooms are golden.
Sprinkle with flour and paprika; cook and stir 3 minutes; add parsley and gradually add stock. Cook and stir until slightly thickened. Cover and simmer 15 minutes. Beat sour cream and egg yolks, whisk in 1/2 cup hot soup and return to rest of soup. Reheat without boiling and adjust seasonings to taste.
Sprinkle with dill or more caraway seeds (if used) and paprika. Serve with buttered pumpernickel squares topped with slices of Monterey Jack or other mild cheese.
Serves 4 - 6

## BOGRACS GULYAS (HUNGARIAN)

4 strips bacon, diced
1 cup minced onions

1 pound lean beef, cut into small cubes
1/2 teaspoon marjoram
1-1/2 teaspoons Hungarian paprika*
1 teaspoon salt
1 teaspoon caraway seed
1/4 teaspoon black pepper
1 finely minced garlic clove
3 tablespoons tomato paste

6 cups rich beef stock

2 cups diced, cooked potatoes

*see glossary

*More than a thousand years ago Magyar shepherds carried supplies of cooked, dried meat cubes to turn their boiling pots of selected vegetables into delicious goulash soup. Hungarian goulash through the years has gained fame as a stew as well as a soup, but who can say where the border between them lies?*

Sauté bacon and onion until onion is golden, stirring often. Push to side of pan.
Raise heat, add meat, cook and stir to brown, adding more bacon fat if needed. Sprinkle with seasonings and garlic, cook and stir 3 minutes, and blend in tomato paste.
Add stock, mix, cover and bring to boil. Simmer 40 minutes or until meat is tender.
Add potatoes, heat, adjust seasonings to taste and serve with an extra sprinkling of paprika.
Serves 6 - 8
Or can also add cubed, cooked carrots, celery and bell pepper.

## TURTLE SOUP

3/4 pound (frozen) turtle meat, cut
  into 1-inch cubes
2 cups water
1/2 teaspoon salt

1 cup chopped onion
4 garlic cloves
1/2 teaspoon black pepper
1/4 teaspoon saffron

6 clams, well scrubbed
1/4 pound raw shrimp, cleaned
2 ounces fresh salmon

4 cups water
1/4 cup cornstarch mixed with
  1/2 cup of cold water
1/2 teaspoon sugar
1 teaspoon salt
1/4 teaspoon pepper
1/2 teaspoon tarragon

1/4 cup dry white wine
2 tablespoons butter bits

slivered green onions

*A real production, but worth it. Not the usual clear type of turtle soup, this recipe is a marvelous starting point for experimenting.*

Blanch thawed turtle meat, rinse and return to clean pot. Add water and salt, cover, bring to boil and skim off surface scum.

Add onion, garlic, pepper and saffron; cover, bring back to boil and simmer until turtle is tender, skimming whenever needed.

Add clams, shrimp and salmon; cook over high heat 15 minutes.

Discard clam shells, strain and reserve liquid. Grind turtle mixture in fine-bladed grinder. It will make about 3 cups; reserve 1 cup, which may be frozen for later use in turtle broth.

Combine and heat 2 cups turtle mixture, water, cornstarch binder, sugar and seasonings. Heat and adjust to taste, adding more water if too strong.

Just before serving add wine, reheat and swirl in butter bits. Sprinkle with a generous amount of slivered green onions.

Serves 6 - 8

*Turtle Broth*

Heat reserved 1 cup turtle mixture with 2 cups water, strain and clarify if desired. Add 2 - 3 cups beef stock and simmer with 3 lemon slices and 6 drops of Tabasco 15 minutes, adding more water if broth is too concentrated. Just before serving add 1/4 cup dry sherry. Or try seasoning with basil, marjoram or rosemary.

## RUSSIAN CABBAGE SOUP

1/2 pound each cubed beef and lean pork butt
1/4 pound diced salt pork

1 small cabbage, finely shredded
2 large tomatoes, peeled and diced
1 cup diced onion
1 bay leaf
1/4 teaspoon pepper
1/2 teaspoon salt
4 cups beef stock made with short ribs
  and marrow bones

*for garnish:*

grated Parmesan cheese or
crisp bacon bits
whipped sour cream

Sauté beef, pork and salt pork to brown slightly.
Add half the cabbage and add remaining ingredients
except garnish. Cover, bring to boil and simmer
1-1/2 hours or until meat is tender. Remove bay
leaf.
Bring to boil, add rest of cabbage and cook until
tender-crisp.
Serve with grated Parmesan cheese, or sprinkle with
bacon bits and pass whipped sour cream.
Serves 4 - 6
Or cook diced potatoes and/or celery root in soup
10 minutes before adding cabbage.

## CHLODNIK (POLISH)

2 - 3 cucumbers, peeled, seeded and
  finely diced (2 cups)
2 cups minced cooked beets
1/4 cup finely minced celery
1 garlic clove
1/4 teaspoon salt

3-1/2 cups sour cream
1 cup half-and-half cream or milk
3 tablespoons minced parsley
2 tablespoons minced chives

salt
pepper

julienne of beet and cucumber
sliced radishes

Mince garlic and crush with salt; combine with
cucumbers and beets. Beat milk or cream and sour
cream and combine with parsley, chives, and
cucumber-beet mixture. Add salt and pepper to
taste, chill and adjust seasonings to taste.
Serve with garnish of beet and cucumber julienne
and sliced radishes.
Serves 4 - 6

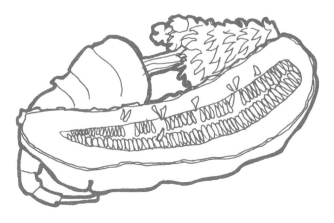

## MIDDLE EAST YOGHURT SOUP

1/2 cup pearl barley
2 cups water

4 cups cold water
2 cups yoghurt (homemade is best)

4 eggs
2 tablespoons flour

2 tablespoons minced onion
2 tablespoons butter
salt

juice from 1 large lemon

minced mint
minced fresh coriander

*It will not surprise me if this soup, suggested by a British friend, does not appeal to every palate. Half the fun of exploring soups is trying the strange ones. After all, there are acquired tastes.*

Cook barley in 2 cups water 1 hour, adding more water if needed. Drain.
Combine cold water and yoghurt. Beat eggs and flour and combine with yoghurt. Bring slowly to simmer and cook 3 minutes.
Add barley, onions, butter and salt to taste; simmer 1 more minute.
Remove from heat and add lemon juice.
Adjust seasonings to taste and pass minced mint and coriander. May be served hot or cold.
Serves 8

## AVGOLEMONO

2 cups half-and-half cream
1-1/2 tablespoons cornstarch
4 cups slightly gelatinous rich chicken stock

6 egg yolks, beaten
1/4 teaspoon paprika
1/8 teaspoon cayenne pepper
1 - 1-1/4 cups lemon juice
salt
pepper

thin lemon slices
minced parsley and/or chives
sieved hard-cooked eggs

Mix cornstarch with a little of the cream, add to rest of cream. Add cream to stock, cook and stir until smooth and slightly thickened.
Whisk 1/2 cup hot soup into egg yolks. Return to rest of soup, beating constantly, and add paprika, cayenne and lemon juice. Adjust seasonings with salt and pepper to taste, strain through fine sieve and chill thoroughly.
Serve in chilled bowls with a garnish of thinly sliced lemon, minced parsley and/or chives, and sieved hard-cooked eggs.
Serves 6
Or heat but do not boil. Add 1 teaspoon grated lemon rind and fold in the beaten whites of two eggs. Serve over hot rice.

# BORSCHT

*Borscht — Borsch — Borsht — Borschdt — Borshch:
More varied by far in its forms than in its spellings.
Older recipes—and some new—call for parsley root,
which seems to be unavailable in any markets. The
one I dug from my garden offered nothing worth-
while.*


## TOMATO BORSHCH (RUSSIAN)

1 cup chopped onions
2 tablespoons butter

1-1/2 cups tomato juice
1-1/2 cups rich brown beef stock
1/2 teaspoon each sour salt* and sugar

1 small head cabbage, finely shredded
1/2 cup shredded cooked meat, preferably
  from stock bones

black pepper
whipped sour cream

*see glossary

Sauté onion in butter until soft and slightly
browned.
Add tomato juice, stock, sour salt and sugar. Cover,
bring to boil and simmer 30 minutes. Strain.
Bring back to boil, add cabbage and cook until
tender-crisp. Reheat with meat and adjust seasonings to taste with sour salt and sugar.
Sprinkle with black pepper and pass a bowl of
whipped sour cream.
Serves 3 - 4

## COLD CLEAR BORSCHT

1-1/2 cups grated raw beets
3 tablespoons grated onion and juice
water to cover (2-1/2 - 3 cups)
1 teaspoon each sour salt* and sugar

1 egg, well beaten

salt
black pepper

whipped sour cream
minced chives

*see glossary

Combine beets, onion, water, sour salt and sugar.
Cover, bring to boil and simmer 30 minutes.
Whisk 1/2 cup hot soup into egg, return to rest of
soup, cook and stir 3 minutes. Do not boil.
Strain, chill and adjust seasonings with salt and pep-
per. Serve in chilled bowls garnished with dollops of
whipped sour cream and minced chives.
Serves 3 - 4

## COLD RUSSIAN BORSHCH

1 16-ounce can tomato juice
3 minced green onions and tops, crushed with
  1/2 teaspoon salt and 2 tablespoons sour cream
1 16-ounce can slivered beets
1 cucumber, peeled, seeded and slivered
2 hard-cooked eggs, sliced
6 radishes, thinly sliced

salt
black pepper

*for garnish:*

minced fresh dill
whipped sour cream

*Spectacular to behold! Typical of the grand manner of the Russian expatriot from whom it came.*

Blend 1/2 cup tomato juice with the green onion-salt-sour cream mixture and combine with rest of ingredients.
Chill and adjust seasonings with salt and pepper.
Serve in chilled bowls with a generous sprinkling of minced fresh dill and pass a bowl of whipped sour cream.
Serves 6
Cooked shrimps may be added.

## EASY RUSSIAN BORSHCH

1 1-1/2-pound brisket of beef or
  meaty, lean short ribs
1 cup chopped onion
1 bay leaf
1 teaspoon salt
6 peppercorns
6 cups water

3 cups coarsely grated beets
1 cup coarsely grated carrots
1 cup diced potatoes
1 8-ounce can tomato purée
3 cups thinly shredded cabbage

minced parsley
whipped sour cream

Combine beef, onion, bay leaf, salt, peppercorns and water. Cover, bring to boil and simmer 3 hours. Strain, cool and chill to remove fat.
Bring stock to boil, add beets, carrots, potatoes and tomato purée. Cook 10 minutes. Add cabbage, bring back to boil, and cook until tender-crisp. Adjust seasonings with salt and pepper and serve sprinkled with minced parsley. Pass a bowl of whipped sour cream.
Serves 6
Or season with red-wine vinegar and sugar to taste.
Add diced meat, if heavier soup is desired.

# CRIMEAN BORSHCH

1/4 cup minced parsley
1 chopped carrot
1 chopped onion
2 chopped leeks, white only
1/2 pound lean salt pork, diced
3 tablespoons butter and/or rendered beef fat

1-1/2 pounds beef brisket or meaty,
  lean short ribs, cut up
8 cups water

6 peppercorns
1 bay leaf
1 teaspoon salt

Sauté parsley, vegetables and salt pork in butter and/or fat until golden. Add meat, water, peppercorns, bay leaf and salt. Cover bring to boil and simmer 2 hours. Strain, reserve and dice meat; set aside. Chill stock and remove fat.

6 beets, shredded
1 carrot, shredded
2 potatoes, diced
1/2 cup rutabagas and/or white turnips, shredded

3 cups finely shredded cabbage
1 cup or more reserved meat
1 teaspoon each sour salt* and sugar
1/4 teaspoon black pepper

2 beets, shredded

minced fresh dill
whipped sour cream

*see glossary

Bring stock to boil, add beets, carrot, potatoes and rutabagas or turnips. Simmer 10 minutes. Add cabbage and reserved meat, bring to boil and cook 5 minutes. Add sour salt, sugar and pepper. Adjust to taste.
Wrap additional 2 shredded beets in cheesecloth and squeeze out as much juice as possible. Add juice only to soup for color.
Reheat and serve sprinkled with lots of fresh dill. Pass a bowl of whipped sour cream.
Serves 10
Or 1 8-ounce can tomato purée may be added for different flavor.

# A Meal in a Bowl

*Drink's bad effects may in a great measure be taken off by a dinner of mutton broth, or soup maigre, on the following day.*
— A. Hunter, "Culina," 1806

Boisterous, medieval knights clutching dripping chunks of meat from a giant bowl may come to mind when thinking of soup as a complete meal. Generally these hearty soups contain chunks of solid food and therefore should be served in broad, shallow bowls with knives and forks as well as spoons.

Sour French bread and sweet butter make ideal accompaniments. Small salads and light desserts go well with these soups, too.

# GUMBO

1 2-pound chicken, cut up
2 tablespoons butter and/or rendered chicken fat
8 cups chicken stock
1 teaspoon paprika
2 garlic cloves
1/2 teaspoon turmeric
1/2 cup celery leaves, chopped
1/4 pound lean ham, cubed
1/2 cup diced celery
1 bunch green onions and tops, chopped
1 leek, chopped
2 tablespoons butter and/or fat
2 tablespoons flour
1 teaspoon paprika
1/2 teaspoon pepper
bouquet garni of:
  8 sprigs parsley
  1 sprig thyme
  1 bay leaf
  4 cloves
  1/2 teaspoon mace or allspice
1/4 pound crab legs
1/4 pound canned or bay shrimp
1 10-1/2-ounce jar oysters, frizzled in butter and
  own juices 3 minutes
1 10-ounce package frozen okra or 1 cup
  fresh, cut up and cooked
salt
pepper
Worcestershire sauce
Tabasco
1 teaspoon filé*

minced parsley
paprika

*see glossary

Brown chicken in butter and/or fat, add stock, paprika, garlic, celery leaves and turmeric. Cover, bring to boil and simmer gently 1 hour or until chicken is tender. Cool, remove chicken from bones, cut up, and reserve. Strain stock.

Brown ham, celery, green onions and leek in butter or fat. Sprinkle with flour, cook and stir 3 minutes, and deglaze with 2 cups of the stock, scraping the bottom of pan. Add rest of stock, pepper, paprika, and bouquet garni. Cover and simmer 1 hour.

Discard bouquet garni. Add crab, shrimp, oysters, okra and reserved chicken. Reheat carefully and adjust seasonings to taste with salt, pepper, Worcestershire sauce and Tabasco. Remove from heat, stir in filé, and sprinkle with minced parsley and paprika. Serve with garlic French bread.

Serves 8 - 10

Or add 2 cups stewed tomatoes or 1 can tomato paste. Serve with bowls of fluffy white rice.

## OYSTER STEW

1/2 cup celery, thinly sliced on diagonal
1 tablespoon minced onion
1/2 teaspoon pressed garlic
2 tablespoons butter
1/2 cup cooked small pasta

1-1/2 pints oysters, drained

1-1/2 pints half-and-half cream
1 cup clam juice

catsup
Worcestershire sauce
black pepper
cayenne pepper
thyme
saffron
dry mustard
tarragon
lemon juice

salt
dry sherry

chopped celery leaves or minced parsley

*Making oyster stew is a matter of personal taste. Choose your own seasonings from those I've suggested. The steamed vegetables and pasta are optional.*

Steam celery, onion and garlic in butter until celery is tender-crisp.
Combine oyster liquor with cream and clam juice and seasonings of choice. Bring just to boil and add oysters and celery-onion-garlic mixture and/or pasta. Bring back to boil and cook only long enough to curl the edges of the oysters. Do not overcook.
Adjust seasonings with salt. Just before serving add sherry.
Garnish with celery leaves or parsley and sprinkle with paprika.
Serves 4
Or if not using the steamed vegetables, swirl in 2 tablespoons butter bits before garnishing.

## COCK-A-LEEKIE

4 cups minced leeks, white part and some of
  tender green
6 cups chicken stock

1 tablespoon rendered chicken fat
1/2 cup pearl barley, cooked in salted
  water 1-1/2 hours

1-1/2 cups shredded, cooked chicken
1 cup half-and-half cream

salt
white pepper

minced parsley

Cook leeks in 3 cups of the stock until tender.
Add fat, drained barley and rest of stock. Cover and cook until barley is mushy.
Add chicken and cream and reheat.
Adjust seasonings with salt and pepper and sprinkle with lots of minced parsley.
Serves 6

132

# HERB OXTAIL SOUP

2-1/2 pounds oxtails, cut up
2 tablespoons butter and/or rendered beef fat
1/2 teaspoon salt
1 teaspoon white pepper

1 cup chopped onion
2 minced garlic cloves
2 teaspoons powdered mushroom
3 cups dry red wine
2 cups water
bouquet garni of:
  2 sprigs parsley
  1 sprig rosemary
  1 sprig thyme
  2 sprigs oregano

1/2 cup pearl barley

1 cup sliced carrots
1 cup diced potatoes
2 cans beef broth
1 can vegetable juice (optional)

1/2 cup Madeira

Brown oxtails in butter and/or fat on all sides, sprinkling with salt and pepper as they are cooking. Add onion and garlic the last turn, brown, sprinkle with powdered mushroom and add wine, water and bouquet garni. Cover, bring to boil and cook 1-1/2 hours.

Cool, chill, remove fat and bring back to boil. Add barley and cook 1-1/2 hours.

Remove bouquet garni, add carrots, potatoes, broth and optional juice. Bring back to boil and cook 15 minutes or until vegetables are tender-crisp. Adjust seasonings.

Just before serving add 1/2 cup Madeira or to taste.
Serves 4 - 6

# THICK OXTAIL SOUP

2-1/2 pounds oxtails, cut up
1 cup chopped onion
3 minced garlic cloves
2 ribs celery, chopped
1 teaspoon salt
7 cups water

1/2 cup pearl barley

1/2 cup lentils

salt
black pepper

minced parsley

Combine oxtails, vegetables, salt and water; cover, bring to boil and cook 1-1/2 hours at medium-high boil. Skim off any scum that rises to the surface.

Cool, chill and defat. Reheat, add barley and cook rapidly 45 minutes, adding water if needed as the barley swells.

Add lentils and cook another 45 minutes until barley and lentils are tender but lentils still hold their shape. Add water if the soup is too thick, reheat, adjust seasonings with salt and pepper and serve with a generous sprinkling of minced parsley.
Serves 4 - 6

## BRAZILIAN BEAN SOUP

2 cups black beans, washed
8 cups hot water
1-1/2 teaspoons salt
1 8-ounce can tomato sauce
1 large onion, minced
1 large garlic clove, minced
2 ounces salt pork, diced

1 or more small, dried hot red peppers
12 ounces fresh pork, cubed
8 ounces Portuguese linguesa sausage
1/4 teaspoon black pepper

*This is a very hot soup; to make it milder, use less red pepper.*

Soak beans in water for 4 hours. Add salt, tomato sauce, onion, garlic and salt pork. Cover, bring to boil and simmer 45 minutes.

Add red pepper, pork, sausage and black pepper. Bring back to boil and simmer until beans are cooked but still hold their shape. Discard peppers. Adjust seasonings to taste and serve with hot French rolls. Pass iced orange slices and watercress sprigs.

Serves 6 - 8

Serve with kale or collard greens and plain rice.

## SPLIT PEA

1-1/2 cups green and/or yellow split peas

3 - 4 ham hocks and/or bones with meat
1 pair pig's feet
2 cups sliced onion
1 cup chopped carrots
2 minced garlic cloves
2 cups chopped celery and leaves
2 tablespoons butter and/or ham fat

12 peppercorns
3 parsley sprigs
1 bay leaf
2 tablespoons fines herbes
6 cups water and juice from canned ham and/or chicken stock

1 can evaporated milk

marjoram
salt
pepper

dry sherry

Brown ham hocks and/or bones, pig's feet and vegetables in butter and/or fat.

Add peas, peppercorns, herbs and water, juice and/or stock. Cover, bring to boil and simmer, stirring occasionally, 3 hours. Remove ham hock and pig's feet.

Force through food mill or sieve, pushing as much pulp through as possible. Reheat with evaporated milk, thin with stock if desired, and adjust seasonings with marjoram, salt and pepper.

Just before serving add dry sherry to taste and serve with cocktail rye.

Serves 6 - 8

For heartier meal, add meat from ham hocks, cooked sausages, browned mushrooms, potato dice and/or vegetable julienne. Sprinkle with grated Parmesan cheese.

## BOUILLABAISSE

3/4 cup minced onion
1/4 cup minced white of leeks
6 minced garlic cloves
1 sprig fennel (if available)
3 sprigs crushed parsley
1 bay leaf
1 3-inch strip of (dried) orange peel

5 - 6 pounds of fresh seafood, some from each of the following categories:

| crustaceans | firm | delicate |
|---|---|---|
| crab | sea bass | whiting |
| shrimp | flounder | red mullet |
| crayfish | grunt | sablefish |
| langoustes | haddock | sole |
| lobster | perch | |
| | scrod | |
| | red snapper | |
| | gray snapper | |
| | sea trout | |
| | rockfish | |
| | halibut | |

1/2 - 3/4 cup olive oil
1 teaspoon salt
1/4 teaspoon freshly ground black pepper
1/4 teaspoon saffron

3 quarts water, fish stock and/or dry white wine — combination of

10 - 12 stale French bread slices, (not toasted or fried)

*Immortalized in Thackery's ballad as "a noble dish —a sort of soup, or broth, or brew" a bouillabaisse is a general category more than a particular soup.*

Put vegetables, herbs and orange peel in large kettle. Arrange selected cleaned crustaceans over vegetables and top with firm fish of choice. Pour olive oil over and sprinkle with salt, pepper and saffron. Add liquid, cover, and bring to fast boil; quick cooking is essential to the consistency. Boil 7 minutes, add delicate fish of choice and cook 6 more minutes. Do not cook more than 15 minutes in all. Place a slice of bread in each bowl. Arrange crustaceans and fish on a platter to be served separately. Adjust flavor of broth and moisten each piece of bread. Serve rest of broth in tureen. Serve with aioli sauce (see page 180), if desired.
Serves 10 - 12
Quartered or sliced potatoes may be added at the same time as the firm fish.

# EAST INDIAN MULLIGATAWNEY

1 2-1/2 - 3-pound chicken, cut up
1 teaspoon paprika
1/2 teaspoon salt
1/4 teaspoon black pepper
3 - 4 tablespoons rendered chicken fat

1/3 cup each diced turnip, carrot, onion, celery,
  and tart peeled apple

1 tablespoon rice flour
1 - 2 teaspoons curry powder

6 cups chicken stock
bouquet garni of:
  1 bay leaf
  3 parsley sprigs
  1 thyme sprig
  6 peppercorns
  2 whole cloves
1/4 cup minced green pepper
1/8 teaspoon mace
1/4 teaspoon black pepper
1 teaspoon salt
1/4 - 1/2 cup tomato paste (optional)
1/4 teaspoon sugar (optional)
lemon rice balls

Sprinkle chicken with paprika, salt and pepper and sauté a few pieces at a time in fat. Remove and set aside.

Add vegetables and apple; stir and cook until golden.

Sprinkle with flour and curry powder, cook and stir 3 minutes, gradually add stock, and cook and stir until smooth. Add chicken, bouquet garni, green pepper and seasonings. Cover, bring to boil and simmer until chicken is tender.

Remove chicken and cut meat into small pieces. Set aside.

Strain broth, forcing as much pulp through sieve as possible.

Heat, adjust seasonings and add tomato paste and sugar if desired.

Serve with lemon rice balls and as much chicken as desired.

Serves 6

Or add puréed canned garbanzo beans and combine thoroughly.

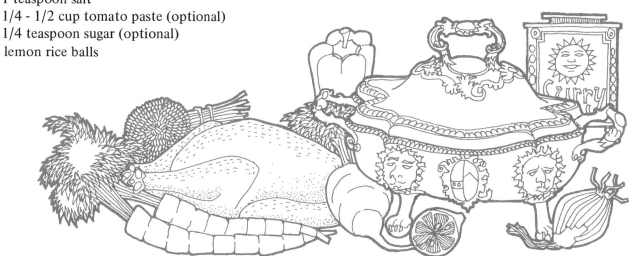

## LEMON RICE BALLS

3/4 cup raw rice, well washed
1-1/2 cups plus 2 tablespoons water
1-1/2 tablespoons lemon juice

1/2 teaspoon freshly grated lemon peel
1/2 teaspoon salt
1/4 teaspoon black pepper

2 - 3 tablespoons garlic olive oil
(let 2 or 3 garlic cloves stand in 1 cup olive
oil overnight — keep on hand!)

Spread rice evenly on the bottom of a saucepan; combine water and lemon juice and add to rice. Let stand at least 1 hour. Bring to boil over high heat, uncovered, and reduce heat slightly. Cook until all the water has evaporated. Cover immediately and cook at lowest heat 30 - 40 minutes. Rice should be sticky but not gooey.

Season with lemon peel, salt and pepper, stirring in with a fork. Adjust seasonings to taste.

When cool enough to handle, form rice into 30 marble-size balls; if it cools off too much you may need to dip your fingers in water. These may be made ahead and kept at room temperature up to 4 hours. Sauté balls in oil, turning several times, until they barely start to turn golden. Do not sauté too long or they will form too much crust. Drain on paper toweling and serve immediately.

## CREAMY MINESTRONE WITH PESTO

2 tablespoons minced onion
1/2 cup minced celery
2 teaspoons olive oil
2 turnips and tops, bulbs minced and tops
finely chopped
1/2 cup finely shredded cabbage
1/2 cup finely chopped beet greens, stems and ribs
removed (or Swiss chard)
1/4 cup minced parsley
1/2 teaspoon salt
1/4 teaspoon black pepper
3 cups rich veal or chicken stock
2 cups half-and-half cream
1 recipe pesto (see below)
salt
pepper
oregano

grated Parmesan cheese

Sauté onion and celery in oil until soft. Add vegetables, parsley, salt, pepper and stock. Cover, bring to boil and simmer 20 minutes until vegetables are tender. Add cream, reheat and adjust seasonings to taste with salt, pepper and oregano. Just before serving drizzle pesto over top and pass Parmesan cheese.
Serves 6

## PESTO

1/4 cup minced fresh basil
1 minced garlic clove
1/2 cup freshly grated Parmesan cheese
1 tablespoon olive oil

Mash basil, garlic and cheese; add oil as needed to make a paste.

## LAMB WITH MINT

3-1/2 - 4 pounds meaty lamb blocks
1 cup dry red wine
4-1/2 cups water
1 onion stuck with 3 cloves
bouquet garni of:
  4 parsley sprigs
  2 savory sprigs
  1 thyme sprig
  1 bay leaf
  6 peppercorns
2 ribs celery and tops, chopped
3 parsnips, diced
2 teaspoons salt
1/2 cup diced celery root
1 package frozen peas
2 tablespoons minced leeks

salt

pepper

1/2 cup minced fresh mint

*A rich luncheon or supper soup to be served in small portions.*

Combine lamb blocks, wine, water, onion, bouquet garni, celery, parsnips and salt. Cover, bring to boil and cook 3 hours until lamb is tender. Remove lamb and cut off enough meat to make 1-1/2 cups. Reserve.
Strain stock, cool and chill to remove fat.
Bring back to boil with celery root, peas and leeks, cover and simmer 15 minutes or until vegetables are soft. Purée in blender.
Add slivered lamb, reheat and adjust seasonings with salt and pepper.
Sprinkle with mint, bring *just* to boil and serve immediately.
Serves 6

## SCOTTISH BROTH

4 cups lamb or veal stock
leftover lamb and bones
2 cups water
3/4 cup pearl barley

1/2 cup diced turnips
3/4 cup diced carrots
1/2 cup diced leeks and
  some green tops
1 cup diced celery

1 cup fresh mushrooms, diced
3 tomatoes, peeled and diced

salt

pepper

*This is a simple, rather bland soup. Serve with a tangy salad and hard rolls.*

Combine stock, leftover lamb and bones, water and barley. Cover, bring to boil and simmer 1/2 hour. Remove meat and bones, shred meat and reserve.
Continue cooking soup 1-1/2 hours or until barley is soft.
Add turnips, carrots, leeks and celery; cook 15 minutes. Add mushrooms and tomatoes and cook 5 more minutes. Add shredded lamb and reheat. Adjust seasonings to taste with salt and pepper. Soup should be thick.
Serves 6 - 8

## SLUMGULLION

1 veal knuckle, blanched
2 large, meaty veal shanks, blanched
8 cups water
1 teaspoon salt
bouquet garni of:
  4 parsley sprigs
  1 marjoram sprig
  1 rosemary sprig
  1 thyme sprig
  1 tablespoon basil
  1 rib celery, cut up
1 onion stuck with 3 cloves

1/4 cup each minced onion and celery
2 tablespoons minced green pepper
1 minced garlic clove
2 tablespoons olive oil
1 cup each diced turnips and carrots
1/2 cup diced celery root
3/4 cup beans, cut on diagonal
1/4 pound pepperoni, sliced

1/2 cup diced potatoes

1/2 package frozen peas, thawed
1/2 package frozen spinach, thawed
2 cups canned tomatoes
2 10-1/2-ounce cans beef broth
1 - 1/2 cups veal cubes (from shanks)

1 cup macaroni shells, cooked

garlic powder
crumbled basil
salt
pepper

grated Parmesan or Romano cheese

Combine veal knuckle, shanks, water, salt, bouquet garni and onion. Cover, bring to boil and simmer 1-1/2 - 2 hours until veal is tender.
Remove shanks and cut meat into cubes; reserve. Strain and cool stock, chill and remove fat.
Sauté onion, celery, green pepper and garlic in oil until soft. Add to stock, bring to boil and add turnips, carrots, celery root, beans and sausage. Bring back to boil and cook 10 minutes.
Add potatoes and cook 5 minutes. Add peas, spinach, tomatoes, broth and reserved meat cubes. Bring to boil and boil 5 minutes; add macaroni, reheat and adjust seasonings to taste with garlic powder, basil, salt and pepper.
Serve with hot French rolls, sweet butter and a robust red wine. Pass grated Parmesan or Romano cheese.
Serves 8 - 10
Just before serving add red wine to taste.

# CREAM OF CHICKEN WITH VEGETABLES

1 2-1/2 - 3 pound chicken
2 cups beef stock
4 cups chicken stock
1 onion stuck with 3 cloves
1 chopped leek
1 chopped carrot
1 cup chopped celery
3 chopped green onions and tops
1 sprig each marjoram and thyme
3 parsley sprigs
1 tablespoon salt
6 peppercorns

1/4 cup each cooked peas, corn, mushrooms
  and cauliflower
3 egg yolks, beaten
1 cup heavy cream
1/2 - 1 cup half-and-half cream
1/2 teaspoon salt
1/4 teaspoon white pepper
1 tablespoon lemon juice
1/4 teaspoon tarragon

grated Cheddar cheese or raw carrot

Combine chicken, stocks, vegetables, herbs, salt and peppercorns. Cover, bring to boil and simmer 1 hour or until chicken is tender. Remove chicken and cool. Strain broth, cool, and chill to remove fat.

Remove meat from chicken, julienne 2 cups of white meat and reserve. Dice 1-1/2 cups dark meat and purée in blender with 1 cup of stock. Return to rest of stock and reheat.

Beat yolks and heavy cream, whisk in 1/2 cup hot soup and return to rest of soup. Add vegetables and chicken white meat. Reheat but do not boil.

Thin with half-and-half cream, season with salt, pepper, lemon juice and tarragon. Adjust seasoning to taste and serve with a garnish of grated Cheddar cheese or grated raw carrot.

Be sure to stir well when serving, as puréed dark meat tends to settle on the bottom.

Serves 6 - 8

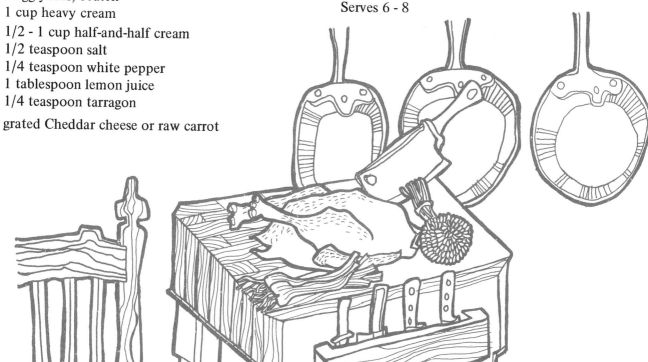

## VEAL PROVENÇALE

2 tablespoons olive oil
2 tablespoons flour
4 cups rich chicken or veal stock

1 cup chopped onion
1 teaspoon minced garlic
1-1/2 pounds lean veal, cut in 1/2-inch cubes
1/2 teaspoon Maggi's seasoning
1/2 teaspoon Beau Monde seasoning
1/2 teaspoon salt
1/2 teaspoon white pepper

1 egg yolk, beaten
2 - 3 tablespoons lemon juice

minced parsley and/or grated Parmesan

Heat oil, sprinkle with flour, cook and stir 3 minutes. Gradually add stock; cook and stir until smooth and slightly thickened.
Add onion, garlic, veal and seasonings. Cover and simmer 30 minutes or until veal is tender.
Adjust seasonings to taste.
Beat egg yolk and lemon juice, whisk in 1/2 cup hot soup and return to rest of soup. Serve immediately sprinkled with minced parsley and/or grated Parmesan.
Serves 4
Or add 1 cup cooked small shell macaroni and/or 1 cup heavy cream.

## TURKEY WITH OYSTERS

2 cups celery, sliced on diagonal
1/2 cup each diced onion and leeks
1 minced garlic clove
1/4 cup butter and/or rendered chicken fat

5 tablespoons flour

2 cups milk or half-and-half cream
3 cups rich turkey stock

2 cups diced leftover turkey
1/2 teaspoon each nutmeg and white pepper
1/2 teaspoon salt
1 teaspoon lemon juice

1 pint oysters
1 tablespoon butter

minced parsley

Sauté celery, onion, leeks and garlic in butter and/or fat until onions are soft.
Sprinkle with flour, cook and stir 3 minutes, and gradually add milk and/or cream and stock. Cook and stir until smooth and thickened.
Add turkey, reheat and season with nutmeg, pepper, salt and lemon juice. Adjust to taste.
Frizzle oysters and their juice in butter until edges curl. Add to hot soup and serve immediately with a generous sprinkling of minced parsley.
Serves 6
Or, finely minced raw celery and leaves enhance the flavor; sprinkle on top.

## MENUDO

2 pounds honeycomb tripe
1 veal knuckle
1 pound maiz cacahuanzincle*

3-1/2 quarts water
1 garlic clove
1/2 teaspoon oregano
3 green onions, cut up
6 peppercorns
1/2 bunch cilantro, stems only, cut up
1/2 teaspoon chili powder
1 teaspoon salt

cilantro sprigs for garnish

*Fermented hominy available in Mexican markets; can be frozen for future use.

*This hearty Mexican cold-weather soup may amaze conventional tripe and hominy lovers. Be prepared for something out of the ordinary. Smooth tripe, which is chewier, may be preferred; it takes 1/2 hour more cooking.*

Blanch tripe, veal knuckle and hominy separately. Cut tripe into 1-inch pieces and set aside.
Combine veal knuckle, hominy and remaining ingredients. Cover, bring to boil and simmer 2 hours.
Add tripe, bring back to boil and cook another hour. Adjust seasonings.
Garnish with cilantro sprigs.
Serves 10 - 12

## ITALIAN BREAD AND CABBAGE SOUP

8 slices stale sour dough bread
6 cups rich beef stock
3 - 5 pressed garlic cloves
1-1/2 cups finely shredded cabbage
3/4 cup finely sliced onion
1 8-ounce can tomato sauce
1/2 teaspoon salt
1/4 teaspoon black pepper
3 tablespoons each grated Parmesan and
   Romano cheese

minced Italian parsley

Cover the bottom of a large Dutch oven or casserole (with a tight lid) with bread, overlapping the slices. Pour in stock and arrange a layer of garlic, cabbage and onion. Spread with tomato sauce and season with salt, pepper and cheeses.
Cover and bake in a 375° oven 45 minutes. Check after 30 minutes and add extra stock if the soup appears to be too thick.
Serve with a generous sprinkling of minced Italian parsley.
Serves 4 - 6

# BOURRIDE

2 pounds fish filets (flounder, bass, red snapper,
   butter fish)  4 filets
8 cups water
1-1/2 cups chopped onion
2 chopped tomatoes
3 parsley sprigs
1 oregano sprig
1 bay leaf
6 coriander seeds
1 cup chopped celery
3 garlic cloves
1 orange peel or 1 teaspoon grated dried orange
   peel
2 teaspoons salt
4 peppercorns
1/4 teaspoon saffron
2 tablespoons olive oil

8 slices stale French bread

salt
black pepper

2 egg yolks, beaten

aioli sauce (see page 180)

Bring water, vegetables, herbs, seasonings and oil to
boil, cover and simmer 20 minutes.

Raise heat, add fish wrapped in cheesecloth, lower
heat and poach gently 10 - 12 minutes until just
tender.

Place a slice of bread into each of 8 bowls, top with
half a filet, and keep warm.

Strain stock and adjust seasonings with salt and
pepper.

Whisk 1/2 cup hot soup into egg yolks and return
to rest of soup.

Ladle soup into bowls and top with 1 tablespoon
aioli sauce for each serving.

Serves 8 generously

# FAMILY MINESTRONE

6 cups stock made with oxtails or leftover
  roast beef
1/4 cup chopped Italian parsley
1/8 teaspoon rosemary

1/4 cup minced leeks
1/2 cup minced onion
1 tablespoon olive oil
1 16-ounce can kidney beans, drained and rinsed

1 cup Swiss chard, cut up
1/2 cup each lima beans, Italian string beans,
  cut up, broccoli flowerets, diced potato and
  chopped celery
3 cups finely shredded cabbage

1/2 cup semolina pasta
1 12-ounce can tomato juice or
  vegetable juice
1/2 cup pearl barley, precooked
1 cup diced meat from bones

salt
pepper
1/2 cup dry sherry

minced Italian parsley
finely minced garlic
grated Parmesan cheese

Simmer stock with parsley and rosemary 20 minutes. Strain.

Sauté leeks and onion in oil 5 minutes. Add to reheated stock with beans and fresh vegetables. Bring to boil and cook until vegetables are almost tender.

Add pasta, cook until tender and reheat with tomato juice or vegetable juice, barley and meat.

Adjust seasonings to taste with salt and pepper, add sherry just before serving and sprinkle with lots of minced Italian parsley and finely minced garlic. Pass grated Parmesan.

Serves 6 - 8

## STUFFED SQUID SPECTACULAR

6 5 - 6-inch squid, cleaned and well dried

2 tablespoons minced onion
1 teaspoon minced garlic
1 tablespoon minced dried mushrooms which have
    first been softened in lukewarm water and dried
2 tablespoons olive oil

1-1/2 tablespoons finely minced parsley
1/2 cup fine bread crumbs
1 tablespoon grated Parmesan cheese
1/4 teaspoon oregano
1/2 teaspoon salt
1/4 teaspoon black pepper

1/2 cup minced celery and leaves
1/4 cup thinly sliced carrot
1/4 cup minced onion
1 minced garlic clove
3 tablespoons minced parsley
3 tablespoons olive oil

2 large tomatoes, peeled and diced
1 teaspoon anchovy paste

1/2 cup white wine

3 cups fish stock
1 cup chicken stock

12 ounces firm white fish, cut into
    2-inch cubes

salt
pepper
Tabasco

*Don't be discouraged by the length of this recipe— once the squid have been prepared, the worst is over! There are a few foods inflation has passed by; squid at 39 cents a pound is one. Perhaps the appearance scares people off, but I rarely find anyone who doesn't like these strange little creatures once he tastes them properly prepared.*

Cut fins off squid and mince finely with the tentacles. Reserve. Set aside squid bodies.

Sauté onion, garlic and mushrooms in oil 5 minutes, stirring to coat well.

Raise heat, add minced fins and tentacles, cook and stir 3 minutes. Remove from heat, add parsley; bread crumbs, cheese and seasonings. Adjust to taste and add more olive oil if too dry.

Stuff squid bodies, leaving 3/4-inch unfilled at end; skewer shut with a toothpick. If done ahead, chill until ready to use.

Sauté vegetables, garlic and parsley in oil 5 minutes; push to one side, raise heat and quickly brown squid on both sides. Remove squid and set aside.

Add tomatoes and anchovy paste; blend thoroughly.

Raise heat, add wine and boil rapidly 5 minutes. Add stocks, bring to boil, and add squid and fish. Cover and cook over medium heat 8 minutes; do not overcook or both the squid and the fish will toughen.

Adjust seasonings with salt, pepper and Tabasco.
Serves 6

# Some Like it Cold

Many people, disenchanted with mere flavoring, sugar, cyclamates, saccharin, malt, hops, alcohol, fizz water, and other nonfoods, are discovering the pleasures of tasty cold soups served around the pool or on the patio as well as in the dining room.

Here you'll find soups that are best cold, along with some equally good hot or cold. Elsewhere other soups, too, suggest serving cold as an option.

Dishes and soup both should be chilled in the refrigerator all day or overnight, and chilled individual bowls or serving bowl should be nested in crushed ice if at all possible. Adjust seasonings *after chilling,* embellish with any of the garnitures that appeal, and serve with toasts, croutons or other accompaniments.

## VICHYSOISSE

1-1/2 cups minced leeks, white and some green
1/4 cup minced onion
1 minced garlic clove
4 tablespoons butter and/or rendered chicken fat

3 cups chicken stock, or combination of
  chicken and beef
1/2 teaspoon powdered mushroom
1/4 teaspoon white pepper
2 cups diced baking potatoes

3 cups milk
1 cup heavy cream

salt
pepper
Lemon Chef*

minced dill or green onion tops

*see glossary

Sauté leeks, onion and garlic in butter and/or fat until soft.
Add stock, seasonings and potatoes; cover, bring to boil and simmer until potatoes are soft.
Purée in blender, add milk and cream, blend well and chill.
Adjust seasonings to taste with salt, pepper and Lemon Chef. Serve with a sprinkle of minced dill or green onion tops.
Serves 6 - 8
Or omit powdered mushroom and season with mace or nutmeg. Sprinkle with paprika and minced chives.

## CUCUMBER VICHYSOISSE

3 tablespoons minced green onions and tops
3 tablespoons minced onion
1 tablespoon minced shallots
1/2 cup minced celery
3/4 cup minced parsley
2 tablespoons butter

3 cups chicken stock
3 cups diced potatoes
1/4 cup minced watercress
1/2 teaspoon thyme

2 cups sour cream
1/4 teaspoon salt
2 drops Tabasco

1 large cucumber, peeled, seeded and
  coarsely grated

half-and-half cream

paprika
minced chives

Sauté green onions, onion, shallots, celery and parsley in butter until vegetables are soft but not brown.
Add stock, potatoes, watercress and thyme. Cover, bring to boil and simmer until potatoes are soft.
Purée in blender, cool and blend in sour cream, seasonings and cucumber. Chill.
Adjust seasonings to taste and thin with cream if needed. Sprinkle with paprika and minced chives.
Serves 6 - 8
Or garnish with extra watercress.

147

# LOBSTER BISQUE

3 tablespoons chopped onion
2 tablespoons minced celery
1 tablespoon minced shallot
2 tablespoons butter
2 tablespoons flour

1-1/2 cups half-and-half cream
1 cup chicken stock
1/4 cup dry white wine

1 tablespoon butter
1 8-ounce lobster tail, minced
1/4 cup heated brandy

1/2 teaspoon salt
1/4 teaspoon white pepper
3 drops Tabasco

milk

paprika
minced chives

Sauté onion, celery and shallots in butter 5 minutes, sprinkle with flour, cook and stir 3 minutes. Gradually add cream, stock and wine; cook and stir until smooth and slightly thickened.
Melt butter to bubbly, add lobster and cook rapidly, stirring, until lobster loses its translucent appearance. Pour brandy over, ignite and let burn down.
Combine lobster and juices with cream sauce, cover and simmer 10 minutes. Purée in blender or sieve. Thin to desired consistency with milk, chill, adjust seasonings to taste, and serve with a sprinkling of paprika and minced chives.
Serves 3 - 4

# CRAB OR LOBSTER CURRY

3 chopped tomatoes
1/2 cup chopped onion
1/4 cup chopped celery
1/4 cup minced parsley
2 tablespoons minced green pepper
1 minced garlic clove
1 bay leaf
1/2 teaspoon basil
1/4 teaspoon tarragon
1/4 cup raw rice
2 tablespoons butter
1 cup chicken stock
1 cup fish stock
1 cup half-and-half cream
1 cup finely minced cooked crab or lobster

1 - 2 teaspoons curry powder
1/4 teaspoon white pepper

crab legs or diced lobster meat
minced chives

Cook tomatoes, vegetables, parsley, garlic, herbs and rice in butter, covered, 10 minutes.
Add chicken stock and cook 30 minutes. Remove bay leaf and sieve.
Combine purée with fish stock, cream and crab or lobster. Heat and add curry and pepper.
Chill, adjust seasonings with salt, and garnish with crab legs or diced lobster meat. Sprinkle with lots of minced chives.
Serves 4 - 6

## AVOCADO WITH PINEAPPLE

1 large ripe avocado
1-1/2 tablespoons lemon juice
1/2 cup crushed canned pineapple, drained
1 cup rich chicken stock
1/8 teaspoon chili powder
1/4 teaspoon salt
1/8 teaspoon white pepper

garlic croutons
minced fresh herbs
freshly ground pepper

Purée all ingredients except croutons, herbs and ground pepper in blender. Chill and adjust seasonings to taste. Serve with garlic croutons and a sprinkle of minced fresh herbs.
Pass the peppermill.
Serves 3
Or serve with extra avocado rubbed gently with lemon juice.

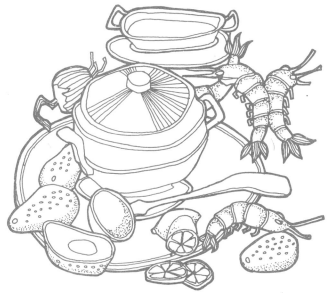

## AVOCADO PURÉE

4 large ripe avocados
2 tablespoons lemon juice
1/2 cup sour cream
2 - 3 tablespoons chicken stock base
3 cups half-and-half cream
1/2 teaspoon salt
1/4 teaspoon white pepper
1/4 teaspoon garlic powder (optional)
1/4 teaspoon onion powder or
1 teaspoon grated onion

*for garnish*
bay or canned shrimp
minced chervil
paprika
freshly ground pepper

Purée ingredients in blender and chill. Adjust seasonings to taste. Serve garnished with bay or canned shrimp, minced chervil and a sprinkling of paprika.
Pass the peppermill.
Serves 4 - 6
Or season with white rum and/or curry; or sprinkle with lots of minced fresh dill.

## COLD ARTICHOKE PURÉE

1 10-1/2-ounce can water-pack artichoke hearts
  (do not use marinated hearts)
1-1/2 cups slightly gelatinous chicken stock
1/4 - 1/2 teaspoon oregano
1/2 teaspoon each salt and chicken stock base
2 tablespoons lemon juice
1/2 cup half-and-half cream
1/2 cup heavy cream

thinly sliced lemon and/or chives
sour cream whipped with soy sauce

*One hot, sunny day a confirmed soup-hater friend accepted a cold cup of this soup with a glassy stare, only to break into a puzzled smile as its refreshing coolness and flavor took effect. Ever since, he's been raving about it, and I think I have another soup convert.*

Drain artichoke hearts and purée in blender with stock and oregano. Pour into saucepan and heat slowly. Season, add creams and adjust to taste. Cool, chill and adjust seasoning.

Serve with garnish of thinly sliced lemon, minced parsley and/or chives and small dollops of sour cream whipped with a little soy sauce.

Serves 3

Pass a tray of crab, bay or canned shrimp, and/or julienned cooked chicken or pork; halved cherry tomatoes; and melba toast.

## PARSLEY VELOUTÉ

2 bunches parsley, tough stalks removed,
   minced (6 cups loosely packed before mincing)
1/4 cup minced onion
2 tablespoons butter and/or rendered chicken fat
1 tablespoon flour
4 cups rich chicken stock

white pepper
cayenne
Lemon Celery*

2 egg yolks, beaten
3 cups half-and-half cream
1/2 - 1 cup heavy cream
salt

sour cream
halved cherry tomatoes


*see glossary

Reserve 1/2 cup parsley for garnish. Sauté rest of parsley and onion in butter and/or fat 5 minutes, stirring to coat. Sprinkle with flour, cook and stir 3 minutes, and gradually add stock. Cook and stir until smooth and slightly thickened. Cover and simmer gently 20 minutes. Purée in blender. Season with white pepper, cayenne and Lemon Celery.

Beat egg yolks and cream, whisk in 1/2 cup hot soup and return to rest of soup. Reheat but do not boil. Cool, chill thoroughly and thin with heavy cream if desired. Adjust seasonings with salt. Serve with dollops of sour cream, reserved parsley and halved cherry tomatoes.

Serves 6 - 8

Or top with minced raw mushrooms which have been sprinkled with lemon juice. Grate a little rind over.

## FRESH GREEN BEAN PURÉE

2 cups each lamb and pork stock
1 pound green beans, cut up

1/2 cup sour cream
1-1/2 cups half-and-half cream
1 teaspoon lemon juice

1/2 teaspoon salt
1/4 teaspoon white pepper
1/8 teaspoon savory

lemon slices
minced parsley

*The lamb and pork stock give the extra flavor!*

Cook beans in stock until tender; purée in blender and cool.

Beat sour cream with a little half-and-half, combine with beans and season with lemon juice, salt, pepper and savory. Add remaining cream.

Chill, adjust seasonings to taste and garnish with lemon slices and minced parsley.

Serves 4 - 6

## SORREL GAZPACHO

3 cups chopped sorrel
3 cups slightly gelatinous, rich chicken stock
1/2 tablespoon chicken stock base
1 minced garlic clove
1 hard-cooked egg, sliced
2 tablespoons lemon juice

1 well-beaten egg

salt, white pepper, paprika

1 large cucumber, peeled, halved, seeded and
  thinly sliced

tomato dice
thinly sliced onion
chopped chervil

Simmer sorrel in stock and stock base, covered, 5 minutes. Remove from heat, add garlic and hard-cooked egg, and cool. Purée in blender and stir in lemon juice.

Pour mixture over beaten egg, beating thoroughly. Add salt, pepper and paprika to taste.

Stir in cucumber and refrigerate at least 4 hours. Serve with seeded, peeled tomato dice, thinly sliced onion, and chopped chervil.

Serves 4

Or add thinly sliced zucchini, minced green onions, julienne of ham, and minced dill and/or chives. May be served without puréeing.

## FRESH ASPARAGUS PURÉE

2-1/2 pounds fresh asparagus, trimmed and washed
1 1-pound can tomatoes
6 cups chicken stock
1 teaspoon basil
1/4 teaspoon white pepper
2 tablespoons flour
1/2 cup sour cream

salt
half-and-half cream

Cut off 20 2-inch tips of asparagus and cut rest into 1-inch pieces. Cook the asparagus and tips, tomatoes, basil and pepper in 2 cups of the stock, removing the tips when they are just tender-crisp.

Reserve the tips for garnish. Continue cooking mixture 20 minutes or until stems are tender; purée in blender.

Combine remaining stock, flour and sour cream with purée; cook and stir until smooth and slightly thickened. Force through medium-fine sieve and add salt to taste. Thin with half-and-half cream if desired. Chill thoroughly, adjust seasoning and garnish with reserved asparagus tips. Serve with curried toast fingers.

Serves 6 - 8

Or garnish with crab legs and/or shrimp and a generous sprinkling of minced parsley and chives.

# GAZPACHO

2 cups gelatinous chicken stock
3 cups water
3 tablespoons chicken stock base
4 garlic cloves
1 large red onion, sliced
1/4 - 1/2 cup minced green pepper

3 large tomatoes, peeled, seeded and
  finely minced
2 tablespoons finely minced green pepper
2 cucumbers, peeled, seeded and finely minced
1 clove garlic, *finely* minced
1-1/2 tablespoons lemon or lime juice
3 tablespoons olive oil
2 - 3 drops Tabasco and/or
1/4 teaspoon cumin
1/4 cup finely minced celery
2 tablespoons finely minced red onion

2 ripe avocados, cut in rings
2 cups herb croutons
extra minced vegetables
minced chives and parsley

*This version of Gazpacho is very mild in comparison to many Spanish recipes. Increase the Tabasco, cumin and garlic for a spicier flavor.*

Bring stock, water, stock base, onion, garlic and green pepper to a boil, simmer gently for 10 minutes, cool, strain and chill.

Gently stir in tomatoes, green pepper, cucumbers, garlic, celery, onion, lemon juice, olive oil, and Tabasco and/or cumin. Chill thoroughly and adjust seasoning to taste.

Serve in large chilled bowls, with an ice cube if desired, and garnish with avocado rings and herb croutons. Pass extra minced vegetables, chives and parsley.

Serves 6

Or add cooked rice or French bread cubes that have been soaked in tomato juice and garlic and diced cooked shrimp. Season with white-wine vinegar to taste.

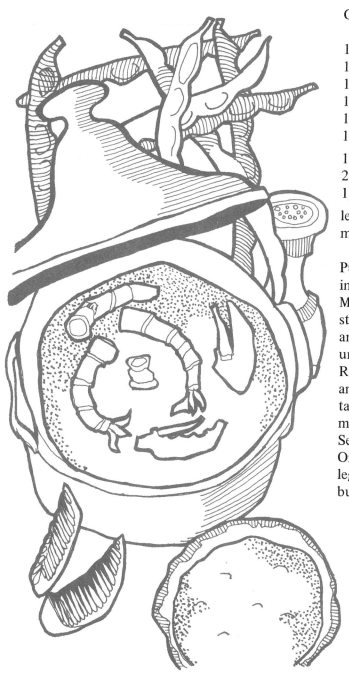

## GREEN BEAN PURÉE

1 1-pound can Blue Lake variety green beans
1 tablespoon chicken stock base
1/2 teaspoon paprika
1/4 teaspoon tarragon
1/4 teaspoon basil
1/8 teaspoon white pepper

1 tablespoon each butter and flour
2/3 cup half-and-half cream
1/2 cup each heavy cream and sour cream

lemon or lime slices
minced green onion tops

Purée beans and their liquid, stock base and seasonings in blender.

Melt butter until bubbly, sprinkle with flour, and stir and cook 3 minutes. Mix bean purée and half-and-half cream; gradually add to roux; stir and cook until smooth and slightly thickened.

Return to blender and combine with heavy cream and sour cream. Cool, chill and adjust seasonings to taste. Serve with lemon or lime slices and lots of minced green onion tops.

Serves 3

Or garnish with bay or canned shrimp and/or crab legs, sprinkle with a little savory, and serve with buttered, toasted English muffins.

## DILLED SOUR CREAM SOUP

5 medium potatoes, peeled and sliced
3-1/2 cups water
1/2 teaspoon each Lemon Dill* and salt

3 cups potato water
1-1/2 cups sour cream, scalded (stir while heating;
 be careful not to scorch)
1-1/2 tablespoons cornstarch mixed with
3 tablespoons cold water
3/4 cups minced *fresh* dill, no stems
3/4 cup sour cream, scalded
2 egg yolks, beaten

salt
white pepper
nutmeg
dill feathers

*see glossary

Cook potatoes, covered, in seasoned water until soft. Drain, reserving 3 cups of potato water (use the potatoes later).
Stir 1-1/2 cups of scalded sour cream into the hot potato water, add cornstarch binder and dill. Boil, stirring constantly, for 3 minutes.
Beat yolks into 3/4 cup scalded sour cream and combine with soup. Do not boil. Season, cool, chill, adjust seasoning and garnish with extra feathers of dill.
Serves 4
Or sprinkle with a little grated lemon peel.

## SPINACH PURÉE

1 pound fresh spinach, coarsely chopped
 (6 - 7 cups loosely packed)
2 cups chicken stock
1/4 cup chopped green onions and tops
1/4 cup minced parsley
1/4 cup minced fresh dill

1 teaspoon chicken stock base
1 cup water
pinch sugar
1/8 teaspoon nutmeg
1/2 teaspoon salt
1/4 teaspoon white pepper
1 cup heavy cream
2 tablespoons dry sherry

cooked, cold lobster
paprika
lemon wedges

Boil spinach in stock 10 minutes. Purée in blender with green onions, parsley and dill.
Dissolve stock base in water, blend with seasonings, spinach mixture, cream and sherry. Chill.
Adjust seasonings to taste and arrange thin slices of cooked cold lobster around edge of bowls. Sprinkle with paprika and serve with lemon wedges.
Serves 4 - 6
Or float a teaspoon of peeled, seeded and coarsely grated cucumber on each portion of soup.

## CUCUMBER MADRILENE

2 cucumbers, peeled, seeded and grated
1/4 cup grated onion
2 teaspoons lemon juice
1/4 - 1/2 teaspoon salt
1/4 teaspoon white pepper
2 - 3 tablespoons minced mint
2 13-ounce cans consommé madrilene
2 cups cooked shrimp
minced mint

*A most refreshing soup—easy to make and lovely to view.*

Finely dice 1 cup of shrimp and combine with rest of ingredients. Chill until set. Serve with remaining shrimp and more minced mint.
Serves 6

## CREAMY PUMPKIN SOUP

1/4 cup minced onion
2 tablespoons minced leeks, white and a little green
2 tablespoons butter

2 cups chicken stock
2 cups (about 12 ounces) fresh pumpkin,* puréed
  after cooking in a little stock
1/2 teaspoon sugar
1/4 - 1/2 teaspoon mace
chicken stock base
white pepper
salt
half-and-half cream

whipped cream

*Off-season, pumpkin can be purchased in Mexican groceries; the type that comes from Puerto Rico is more delicate than ours.

Sauté onion and leeks in butter until soft. Add chicken stock and pumpkin; mix well and heat. Purée in blender and force through sieve.
Add seasonings, chill thoroughly and adjust seasonings to taste. Thin with cream if desired and serve with dollops of whipped cream.
Serves 4 - 6
Or garnish with coriander sprigs.

WATERCRESS

2 tablespoons minced onion
2 teaspoons butter
1-1/2 cups watercress, or 2 cups curlycress leaves
  and tender stems, chopped

1-1/2 teaspoons flour
1/2 teaspoon chicken stock base
1/4 teaspoon white pepper
1/4 teaspoon garlic powder
1 egg
2 cups chicken or veal stock

1/2 cup half-and-half cream
1/2 cup heavy cream

salt

lemon slices
1 hard-cooked egg, sieved

Sauté onions in butter until soft. Purée in blender
with watercress, flour, stock base, pepper, garlic
powder, egg and 1 cup of the stock.
Combine with rest of stock and half-and-half cream.
Cook in double boiler or heavy saucepan 30 minutes, stirring occasionally. Add heavy cream.
Chill, adjust seasonings with salt and garnish with
lemon slices and hard-cooked egg.
Serves 2 - 4
To serve hot, reheat without boiling, adjust seasonings with salt and garnish with lemon slices and
watercress sprigs.

# ZUCCHINI PURÉE

1-1/2 pounds diced zucchini (4 cups)
1/2 cup diced onion
1/2 teaspoon sugar
1/4 teaspoon salt
1/4 teaspoon oregano
2 sprigs chervil
1 cup chicken stock

1 tablespoon butter
1 tablespoon flour
1-1/2 cups milk
1/2 cup stock from zucchini

1 cup heavy cream

salt
white pepper

crab legs
lemon slices
chervil sprigs

Cook zucchini, onion, seasonings and chervil in stock until vegetables are tender. Strain, reserving the liquid, and purée vegetables in blender.

Melt butter until bubbly, add flour and cook and stir 3 minutes. Gradually add milk and 1/2 cup reserved stock; cook and stir until smooth and slightly thickened. Add purée, blend well and stir in heavy cream.

Cool, chill, adjust seasonings with salt and pepper and garnish with crab legs, sliced lemon and chervil sprigs.

Serves 4

To serve hot, thicken with 1 cup fresh peas, cooked and puréed; substitute half-and-half cream for the heavy cream, and heat without boiling. Serve with lemon slices and garlic croutons.

## CREAMY SQUASH SOUP

2-1/2 - 3 cups diced yellow or banana squash
1-1/2 cups diced onion
1/2 cup diced celery
2 tablespoons diced carrot
1 teaspoon basil
2 tablespoons butter

2-1/2 cups chicken stock

1 cup half-and-half cream
1/2 cup heavy cream

1/4 teaspoon sugar
1/8 teaspoon powdered cloves
1/8 teaspoon mace
1/4 teaspoon white pepper
1/2 teaspoon salt

minced chives
paprika

Cook and stir vegetables and basil in butter 10 minutes.
Add stock, cover, bring to boil and simmer until vegetables are tender.
Purée in blender, add creams and heat with seasonings; do not boil.
Cool, chill and adjust seasonings.
Sprinkle with paprika and chives.
Serves 4 - 6
To serve hot, heat with a chiffonade of sorrel, spinach and lettuce (see page 180); or add oysters frizzled in butter and their own juices.

## POTATO-CELERY ROOT

1 cup each diced celery root and potato
1/2 cup minced onion
1/4 cup minced celery
2 tablespoons minced leeks
2 tablespoons minced parsley
2 tablespoons butter

4 cups chicken or veal stock
1/4 teaspoon black pepper
2 bay leaves

2 egg yolks, beaten
1 cup half-and-half cream

1/2 cup heavy cream

salt

drained, minced capers

Sauté vegetables and parsley in butter, stirring to coat well, 5 minutes.
Add stock, pepper and bay leaves. Cover, bring to boil and simmer until vegetables are soft. Discard bay leaves and purée vegetable mixture in blender. Reheat.
Beat egg yolks and half-and-half, whisk in 1/2 cup hot soup and return to rest of soup. Cool, add heavy cream and chill.
Adjust seasonings with salt and serve with capers.
Serves 4 - 6
To serve hot, omit heavy cream and increase half-and-half cream to 1-1/2 cups. Garnish with minced celery leaves.

# CUCUMBER PURÉE

3 large cucumbers, peeled, seeded and diced
1 large onion, diced
3 tablespoons butter

2-1/2 tablespoons flour
1/2 teaspoon paprika
1/4 teaspoon each white pepper and Lemon Celery*
1/4 teaspoon basil or thyme
5 cups rich chicken stock
1/2 tablespoon lemon juice
2 tablespoons dry sherry or dry white wine
1 cup heavy cream

6 lemon slices
1/2 cup peeled, seeded, minced cucumber
2 tablespoons minced fresh dill

*see glossary

Sauté cucumbers and onion in butter until slightly browned.
Sprinkle with flour, cook and stir 3 minutes, add seasonings, and gradually add 2 cups of the stock. Cook and stir until smooth and slightly thickened. Cover and simmer 20 minutes.
Purée in blender, add remaining stock, reheat to blend, cool, and add lemon juice, sherry or wine, and cream. Chill and adjust seasonings to taste with salt, lemon juice and wine. Garnish with lemon slices, cucumber and dill.
Serves 6
To serve hot, omit heavy cream, add 1 cup half-and-half cream, and heat without boiling. Adjust seasonings and garnish with sour cream whipped with a little soy sauce, lemon slices and finely minced green pepper.

# CARROT CRÈME

4 - 5 cups sliced carrots
2 tablespoons chopped onion
1/2 teaspoon each sugar and marjoram
1/4 teaspoon thyme
2 tablespoons butter

2 tablespoons flour
2 cups milk
1 bay leaf
1 tablespoon chicken stock base
2 cups half-and-half cream
1/2 cup heavy cream

salt

minced mint

Steam carrots, onion and seasonings in butter, covered, until carrots are tender.
Sprinkle with flour, cook and stir until browned slightly, and gradually add milk, stirring until smooth. Add bay leaf, cover and simmer gently 30 minutes, stirring occasionally.
Discard bay leaf and purée soup in blender. Add chicken stock base and creams; reheat without boiling.
Chill, adjust seasonings to taste and sprinkle with minced mint.
Serves 4 - 6
Serve hot garnished with plenty of grated raw carrot and minced chervil.

# CREAM OF TOMATO

2 cups canned or fresh tomatoes, chopped
1/2 cup chopped celery
1/4 cup each chopped carrot and onion
1 teaspoon sugar
1/2 teaspoon basil
1 parsley sprig
1 marjoram sprig
1 bay leaf
1 tablespoon sweet butter
1/2 cup chicken stock
1 tablespoon chicken stock base

2 tablespoons butter
2 tablespoons flour
2 cups half-and-half cream
1/4 teaspoon paprika
1/4 teaspoon white pepper

1/4 cup sour cream
salt
basil
tomato dice, seeded and peeled *or*
1/4 cup mayonnaise seasoned to taste with
  curry powder
2 tablespoons minced parsley

Simmer tomatoes, celery, carrot, onion, sugar, herbs and butter in stock and stock base until vegetables are soft. Discard marjoram sprig and bay leaf; force vegetables through food mill.

Melt butter until bubbly, add flour, cook and stir 3 minutes. Gradually add cream; cook and stir until smooth and slightly thickened.

Add vegetable purée, paprika and pepper; simmer, stirring occasionally, 20 minutes.

Blend in sour cream and heat just to melt; do not boil. Cool, chill and adjust seasonings with salt and basil. Garnish with peeled, seeded tomato dice or dollops of curry-flavored mayonnaise and minced parsley.

Serves 6

To serve hot simply heat without boiling, adjust seasonings and garnish with minced artichoke hearts and a sprinkling of minced fresh basil.

# Fruit Soups

*Only the pure in heart can make a good soup*
*—Beethoven, 1824*

Fruit soups are especially popular in Germany as desserts and in the Scandinavian countries for breakfast and lunch. Fruit soups should all be icy cold and served in chilled bowls. Combinations of fresh and dried fruits offer varying degrees of sweetness and tartness. I've found that if a fruit soup is too syrupy or tart it's better to add light wine than more water. A dash of liqueur with its own bite can add an interesting contrast, too.

## SCANDINAVIAN FRUIT SOUP

1 12-ounce package mixed dried fruits, or any
  combination desired
1/2 cup golden seedless raisins
2 tablespoons dried currants
5 cups water

1 orange, sliced 1/4-inch thick
1 lemon, sliced 1/4-inch thick
1/2 cup each currant jelly and sugar
2 tablespoons quick-cooking tapioca
1/4 teaspoon salt
2-1/2 cups unsweetened pineapple juice
1 cup peeled, diced apple (optional)

*An especially attractive soup—marvelous for brunch!*

Combine fruits, raisins, currants and water. Cover, bring to boil and cook until tender.
Add remaining ingredients and simmer 10 minutes. Cool, chill and serve with hard French rolls and sweet butter.
Serves 8 - 10
Or add 1/2 cup or more port.

## PLUM SOUP

1-1/2 cups chopped plums
1/4 cup crumbled rusks
1/2 cup each dry white wine and apple juice
small pinch cinnamon, cloves and ginger

2 tablespoons heavy cream
1 teaspoon sugar
1/2 teaspoon lemon juice
1/4 cup Rhine wine

apple slices rubbed with lemon juice

Cook plums, rusk crumbs, wine, apple juice and spices until plums are soft. Sieve.
Add cream, sugar, lemon juice, and wine. Chill and adjust seasonings to taste, adding more chilled wine if desired.
Garnish with thin slices of unpeeled apple rubbed with lemon juice to prevent discoloring.
Serves 3 -4

## ICY WATERMELON SOUP

1/2 medium watermelon
1 - 1-1/2 cups Rhine wine
2/3 cup sugar
3/4 cup water
4 slices lemon or lime
1 2-inch piece vanilla bean
finely minced mint

Scoop 12 balls from seedless portion of watermelon. Combine with wine and chill.
Simmer sugar, water, lemon or lime slices and vanilla bean, covered, 20 minutes. Discard lemon slices and vanilla bean.
Put 2 cups watermelon cubes, seeds removed, in blender; pour in sugar water and blend until smooth.
Chill, combine with melon balls and wine, and adjust to taste.
Sprinkle with finely minced mint.
Serves 6

## CANTALOUPE SOUP

1 large cantaloupe, diced
5 tablespoons butter
2 teaspoons sugar
1 teaspoon freshly grated lemon rind
1/16 teaspoon powdered ginger
pinch salt
2-1/2 cups milk
white rum and/or lemon juice
sprigs of mint

Reserve 1 cup diced cantaloupe (or scoop out balls) for garnish.
Sauté remainder in butter with sugar, lemon rind, ginger and salt until soft.
Add milk, bring to boil and simmer 10 minutes.
Purée in blender, cool and chill. Adjust seasonings with lemon juice and/or rum.
Garnish with reserved cantaloupe and sprigs of mint.
Serves 4

## RASPBERRY SOUP

1 10-ounce package frozen raspberries, thawed
1 11-ounce can mandarin oranges and juice
1/2 cup orange juice
1/4 cup dry red wine
1/4 cup lemon juice
1 cup Chablis
1 tablespoon kirsch
finely minced mint
mint sprigs

*Pretty and refreshing!*

Combine ingredients and chill.
Adjust to taste with additional sugar, lemon juice and/or wine or kirsch.
Sprinkle with finely minced mint and garnish with mint sprigs.
Serves 6

# GARLIC WITH FRUIT

3 - 5 minced garlic cloves
1/3 cup slivered blanched almonds
3 slices white bread, crusts removed, diced
2-1/2 tablespoons olive oil
3-1/2 cups chicken or veal stock
1/2 teaspoon salt
1/4 teaspoon white pepper
2 tablespoons dry white wine

1/2 cup cantaloupe balls, chilled
1 bunch seedless white grapes, chilled
1/4 pound proscuitto ham, torn into strips

slivered almonds

Purée garlic and almonds in blender and sauté with bread in oil until golden.
Add stock, salt and pepper and cook 10 minutes. Return to blender and purée. Cool.
Add wine, chill and adjust seasonings to taste.
Garnish with melon balls, grapes and ham and pass toasted, blanched slivered almonds.
Serves 4 - 6
Or can use Crenshaw melon instead of cantaloupe

# STRAWBERRY-WINE SOUP

2 cups sliced fresh strawberries
6 tablespoons sugar
1 cup water

2 teaspoons cornstarch mixed with
1 tablespoon cold water

1 cup dry white wine
1 - 2 tablespoons lemon juice
2 teaspoons grated lemon peel

cognac

lemon peel strips

Combine strawberries, sugar and water; simmer until berries are soft.
Stir in cornstarch binder and cook and stir until thickened. Purée in blender.
Add wine, lemon juice and lemon peel. Chill and season to taste with lemon juice, wine and cognac.
Garnish with tiny lemon peel strips.
Serves 4
Or can also purée with 1/4 cup sour cream.

# FRUIT BOUILLON

1 pound fresh bing cherries, pitted and chopped
6 tablespoons orange juice
1-1/2 tablespoons lemon juice
1/4 cup dry sherry

Rhine wine, well chilled

orange and lemon slices

Purée 1/2 cup cherries with the orange juice in blender. Combine with lemon juice and sherry. Add remainder of chopped cherries.
Chill, add wine to taste and adjust, adding sugar if needed.
Float thin slices of orange and lemon on top.
Serves 4

# TOMATO-ORANGE SOUP

2 cups each tomato and orange juice
1/2 cup dry white wine
2 tablespoons lemon juice
1/4 teaspoon minced fresh basil
salt
cayenne pepper
black pepper

whipped cream
minced chives

Combine juices, wine and basil. Chill, adjust with salt, cayenne and pepper. Garnish with dollops of whipped cream and minced chives.
Serves 4 - 6

## BRANDIED PEACH & PLUM SOUP

2 cups each diced fresh peaches and plums
1-1/2 cups each water and dry red wine
2/3 cup sugar
1 slice lemon
1 4-inch cinnamon stick

2 tablespoons cognac

finely minced mint

Cook peaches, plums, water, wine, sugar, lemon and cinnamon, covered, until fruits are soft. Discard lemon and cinnamon; force fruits through sieve.
Add cognac, chill and adjust to taste, adding sugar and/or cognac as needed.
Garnish with finely minced mint.
Serves 6

## MIXED FRUIT SOUP

4 cups diced fresh fruit (plums, apricots, cherries, apples, peaches)
3 cups water
3 tablespoons sugar
2 slices lemon
1 4-inch cinnamon stick

2 tablespoons raspberry juice
1/4 cup orange juice
2 teaspoons lemon juice

6 tablespoons port
sugar

sour cream
mint sprigs

Cook fruit, water, sugar, lemon slices and cinnamon, covered, until fruit is soft. Discard lemon and cinnamon; force fruit through sieve.
Add juices and port; chill and adjust to taste with juice, sugar and/or port.
Serve with dollops of well-whipped sour cream and garnish with mint sprigs.
Serves 6

## COLD CHERRY SOUP

2-1/4 cups water
3/4 cup extra-fine sugar
1 3-inch cinnamon stick
4 cups pitted sour cherries, or
2 1-pound cans water-pack sour cherries, drained

1 tablespoon cornstarch
2 tablespoons water
1/4 cup each dry red wine and heavy cream

Cherry Heering to taste (1/2 cup or more)

mint

Bring water, sugar, cinnamon and cherries to boil. Simmer 30 minutes for fresh, 10 for canned. Mix cornstarch and water, stir into cherries and cook and stir until clear and slightly thickened. Remove about a cup of cherries and some juice; purée in blender and return to rest of soup. Cool, add wine and cream, blend and chill thoroughly.
Just before serving add chilled Cherry Heering to taste; serve in chilled bowls garnished with mint.
Serves 6 - 8
Or serve with dollops of whipped sour cream.

## APFELSUPPE

4 large tart apples, cored and diced
4 slices lemon
1 1-inch cinnamon stick
2-1/2 cups water

1/2 cup sour cream, beaten (at room temperature)
3 - 4 tablespoons extra-fine sugar

1-1/2 cups claret or rosé wine
1 - 2 teaspoons lemon juice

cinnamon
mint sprigs

Cook apples, lemon and cinnamon in water until apples are soft.
Remove lemon, and cinnamon stick and sieve apples, forcing as much pulp through as possible.
Beat 1/2 cup apple mixture with sour cream and return to rest of soup. Add sugar and blend well.
Gradually stir in wine, add lemon juice and chill. Adjust with more sugar, wine and/or lemon juice. Sprinkle with a little cinnamon and serve with a garnish of mint sprigs.
Serves 4 - 6

## RHUBARB FRUIT SOUP

3/4 cup extra-fine sugar
4 cups water
1 3-inch cinnamon stick
3/4 cup dried apricots, cut in 4ths
2-1/2 - 3 cups diced rhubarb

2 tablespoons cornstarch
3 tablespoons cold water
1 package frozen raspberries, thawed and drained
1 tablespoon lemon juice

grated orange rind
sliced strawberries

Combine sugar, water, cinnamon and apricots. Bring to boil, cover and simmer 5 minutes. Add rhubarb, bring back to boil and simmer until rhubarb is barely tender.
Mix cornstarch and water (or use juice from drained raspberries) and add to fruit; cook and stir until slightly thickened and clear. Add raspberries and lemon juice; adjust sugar to taste. Chill.
Garnish with grated orange rind and strawberries.
Serves 6 - 8

## APRICOT WINE SOUP

2/3 cup dried apricots
2/3 cup peeled, diced tart apple
1 cup water

1 12-ounce can apricot-orange nectar
1-1/4 cups apple juice
1/2 cup sour cream

3/4 cup chilled dry white wine

mint sprigs

Cook apricots and apple in water, covered, until apricots are soft, adding more water if needed.
Purée in blender with nectar, apple juice and sour cream.
Chill, add wine to taste, and serve with sprigs of mint.
Serves 6 - 8
Or for extra bite, add a few drops of Tabasco.

# Mini Recipes

Though I feel a cook can make the best soups and derive the most satisfaction by starting from scratch, I'm not a purist in this matter.

There is no reason why one shouldn't take advantage of factory-prepared foods when time is short or the larder is low. There are many ways of adding a personal touch, however, and of making a good commercial product into something even better. Check the garnitures for other ideas, and endless combinations.

1. Add 1/8 teaspoon basil and 1/4 cup dry red wine or Madeira to black bean soup. Garnish with lemon slices.

2. Combine 1 can each cream of tomato and black bean soup with 1-1/2 soup cans water. Heat and serve topped with grated onion and lemon slices.

3. Substitute 1/2 cup rosé wine for part of the water to be mixed with cream of chicken soup. Garnish with lime slices.

4. Lace green turtle or beef or chicken broth with dry sherry. Sprinkle with chives or shredded Cheddar cheese.

5. Combine and heat 1 can each cream of mushroom and asparagus (or tomato and pea), 1 cup each milk and half-and-half cream and 1 cup flaked crabmeat. Just before serving add 1/4 cup dry sherry and 2 tablespoons butter.

6. Combine and heat 3 cans cream of celery soup, 2-1/2 soup cans half-and-half cream, 1 cup shrimp, lobster or crab, and 1/2 cup shredded mild Cheddar cheese. Garnish with sliced black or stuffed olives.

7. Simmer 3 cans beef consommé and 1 soup can water with 12 parsley sprigs 30 minutes. Remove parsley, chill until firm, and break up with fork into chilled bowls. Serve with sour cream and black caviar.

8. Bring 1 can beef broth, 2 cups tomato juice, 1 teaspoon Worcestershire sauce and 2 tablespoons lemon juice just to boil. Cool, chill and serve icy cold garnished with julienned pickled beets and shredded lobster.

9. Combine and heat 3 cans green turtle broth, 2 cans pea soup, 1/2 teaspoon basil and 1 - 2 tablespoons lime juice, Madeira or dry sherry. Pour into ovenproof bowls and top with whipped cream. Broil to brown cream.

10. Heat equal amounts of clam and tomato juice. Garnish with lime slices.

11. Heat 1-1/2 cups vegetable juice, 1/2 cup pineapple juice, 1/2 teaspoon Worcestershire sauce and 3 drops Tabasco. Sprinkle with minced chives or green pepper.

12. Sauté 1/4 cup minced onion in 2 tablespoons butter until soft. Add and heat 2 cans cream of vegetable soup, 1-1/2 soup cans milk and 1 cup minced shrimp. Add 1/2 cup fresh tomatoes, peeled, and diced; reheat briefly and sprinkle with minced dill.

13. Defrost cream of shrimp soup, heat and season with curry powder to taste. Serve hot or cold with minced chervil.

14. Follow package directions for dry leek and onion soup; add 1 can minced clams and juice, reheat and garnish with finely minced raw garlic.

15. Combine 1 can beef consommé or madrilene, 1/2 cup diced shrimp, 1/4 cup minced celery, 2 tablespoons chopped watercress and black pepper to taste. Chill until firm, break up with fork and serve with lemon wedges and watercress.

16. Purée 1/2 cup milk and 1 cup chopped cooked broccoli in blender. Mix with 1 can frozen cream of potato soup, thawed, and 1 cup milk. Heat and serve with lemon slices and garlic croutons.

17. Heat 1 can madrilene and 2 tablespoons sherry. Cool, chill until firm and serve with avocado rings.

18. Sauté 1/4 cup minced onion and 2 tablespoons minced green pepper in 1 tablespoon butter until soft. Combine with 1 can frozen cream of shrimp soup, thawed, 1 soup can milk, 1/2 cup cooked fish and 3/4 cup cooked rice. Heat. Sprinkle with paprika and finely minced green onion tops.

19. Heat 1 can each frozen oyster stew and cream of mushroom soup, 2 cups milk, 1/2 cup cooked cut green beans, 1/4 cup chopped fresh tomatoes, 2 tablespoons minced parsley, 1/4 teaspoon thyme and 1/4 teaspoon white pepper. Sprinkle with paprika and minced chives.

20. Purée in blender 1 can each oyster stew and cream of mushroom soup. Combine and heat with 2 cups milk. Cool, chill and serve in chilled bowls, garnished with chopped or sieved hard-cooked eggs and minced parsley.

21. Combine and heat 1 can each cream of chicken and cream of celery soup and 2 soup cans milk. Cool, chill and garnish with chopped, peeled and seeded cucumber, fresh mint or chopped celery leaves.

22. Sauté 1/2 pound sliced mushrooms, 1/2 cup minced onion and 6 parsley sprigs in 1 tablespoon butter until soft. Add 5 cups chicken stock, cover, bring to boil and simmer 40 minutes. Strain, reheat, add 1/4 cup dry sherry and garnish with sautéed mushroom caps and lemon wedges.

23. Season beef consommé with lemon juice and garnish with lemon slices. Add dry white wine just before serving.

24. Purée in blender 2 cups chilled tomato juice, 1/2 teaspoon salt, 1/4 teaspoon each pepper and basil, 1/8 teaspoon marjoram and 1/3 cup sour cream. Chill and garnish with minced chives and lemon slices. Serve in chilled bowls.

25. Heat 6 cups chicken broth, 1/4 teaspoon grated lime peel and 3 tablespoons lime juice. Garnish with lime slices.

26. Combine and heat 1 can cream of mushroom soup, 1 can frozen lobster bisque, thawed, and 2-1/2 cups milk. Cool, chill and serve with lemon slices and parsley.

27. Combine and heat 1 can each cream of vegetable, pea and tomato soup and 2 cups milk. Garnish with pimiento slivers.

28. Combine and heat 1 can condensed cream of mushroom soup, 1 can condensed chicken vegetable soup, 1 soup can water and 1 12-ounce can whole kernel corn, drained. Add 1/2 cup each half-and-half cream and dry sherry. Sprinkle with bacon bits and minced parsley.

29. Boil 1/2 cup rice in 5 cups chicken stock 15 - 20 minutes. Beat 2 egg yolks with 1/2 cup heavy cream, whisk in 1/2 cup hot soup and return to rest of soup. Reheat without boiling and add 2 - 3 tablespoons port. Sprinkle with parsley.

30. Heat beef consommé with chopped celery stalks and leaves 20 minutes. Strain and serve with celery mince and paprika.

31. Combine and heat 1 can mushroom soup, 1 can creamy corn and 1-1/2 cups milk. Garnish with red bell pepper slivers.

32. Combine and heat 1 can each cream of celery and cream of tomato soup and 1-1/2 cans milk. Serve with sliced cooked frankfurters.

33. Combine and heat 1 can each clam chowder and chicken gumbo and 1-1/2 cans milk or cream. Garnish with minced chives and paprika.

34. Combine and heat 1 can each cream of tomato, green pea and beef broth, 1 can water and 1 cup crab, minced clams or diced shrimp. Just before serving add 3 tablespoons dry sherry and garnish with sour cream dollops or grated sharp Cheddar cheese.

35. Combine and heat 1 can each cream of mushroom and chicken soup, 1 can consommé and 1-1/2 cups evaporated milk. Force through sieve and season with curry powder to taste. Serve hot or cold sprinkled with minced chives.

36. Combine 2 cans consommé, 3/4 cup minced shrimp, 1/4 cup thinly sliced celery, 2 tablespoons each minced parsley and watercress and 1/8 teaspoon white pepper. Chill and garnish with lime wedges, extra whole shrimp and parsley.

37. Combine and heat 1 can frozen clam chowder, thawed, 1 can cream, 1 can green pea soup, 1 can water, 3/4 cup drained canned corn, and 3 tablespoons minced pimiento. Garnish with finely minced raw bell pepper.

38. Purée 1 can each cream of mushroom and cream of chicken soup, 1 small can mushrooms, drained, 2 10-1/2-ounce packages frozen chopped spinach, thawed, 2 teaspoons onion flakes and 1/4 teaspoon minced garlic. Combine and heat with 2-1/2 cups milk and salt and pepper to taste. Garnish with sliced hard-cooked eggs and paprika.

39. Blend 3 eggs, 1/4 cup dry sherry, 1/8 teaspoon nutmeg or mace and 2 tablespoons lemon or lime juice. Slowly pour in 3 cups hot chicken broth and blend 1 minute. Garnish with minced chervil and dice of artichoke heart.

40. Serve jellied consommé or madrilene with crumbled Roquefort cheese and minced chives.

41. Purée 1 10-1/2-ounce package frozen chopped spinach, thawed and drained, 1 26-ounce can vichysoisse, 2 teaspoons chicken stock base, 1 teaspoon onion powder, 1/4 teaspoon garlic powder and 1/2 cup milk. Season with salt and pepper and serve with sieved hard-cooked eggs or grated cucumber.

42. Combine 1 can cream of tomato soup, 1 cup milk, 1/2 cup heavy cream, 2/3 cup creamy cottage cheese, 1/2 teaspoon Worcestershire sauce, and Tabasco and salt to taste. Chill, adjust seasoning and serve in chilled bowls, garnished with slivered green onions.

43. Purée 1 can cream of celery soup, 1 cup milk, 1/2 cup heavy cream, 2 cups firmly packed watercress leaves and some stems and 1 cup peeled, seeded and chopped cucumber. Add salt to taste, chill, adjust seasoning and serve in chilled bowls, garnished with minced watercress.

44. Purée 1 cup tomato juice, 3 tablespoons minced parsley, 3 tablespoons minced onion, 1 peeled and diced tomato, 3 tablespoons sour cream and 1/2 can consommé. Chill, stir and season with Tabasco and Worcestershire sauce and serve in chilled bowls.

45. Purée 2 cups peeled, seeded and diced cucumber, 3 green onions, 2 tablespoons minced parsley, 1 tablespoon fresh dill, 2 cups buttermilk and 1/4 cup sour cream. Chill. Season with salt, serve in chilled bowls and pass the peppermill.

46. Keep this base in the refrigerator (or freezer) for a quick cold soup: Cook 5 cups sliced carrots and 2 tablespoons raw rice in 4 cups bouillon (or 2 each bouillon and consommé) until carrots are soft and rice is tender. Purée in blender and refrigerate. When ready to serve, thin to desired consistency with milk and/or half-and-half cream. Season to taste with salt, pepper, Worcestershire sauce and Tabasco. Garnish with minced chives or grated raw carrot and parsley sprigs. Or thin with milk and sour cream.

# Accoutrements

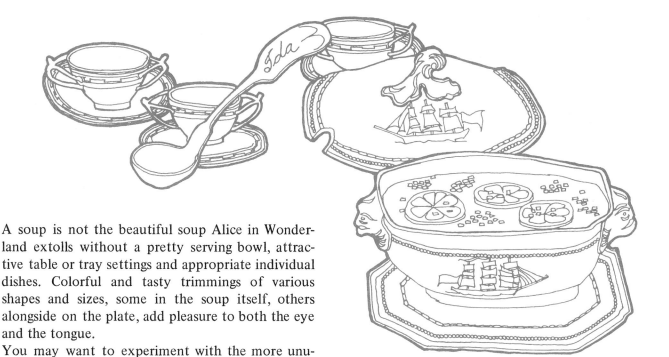

A soup is not the beautiful soup Alice in Wonderland extolls without a pretty serving bowl, attractive table or tray settings and appropriate individual dishes. Colorful and tasty trimmings of various shapes and sizes, some in the soup itself, others alongside on the plate, add pleasure to both the eye and the tongue.

You may want to experiment with the more unusual suggestions that follow before actually serving them to guests.

Cook and try a dumpling or meatball first so you can adjust seasonings to your taste before cooking the entire batch.

## POTATO DUMPLINGS

3 medium potatoes, boiled soft and
  refrigerated overnight
1/4 cup flour
1 egg, beaten fluffy
1/2 teaspoon salt
1/4 teaspoon nutmeg or oregano
1 tablespoon *finely* minced parsley

Grate the potatoes to make about 2-1/2 cups.
Mix in flour, egg, seasonings and parsley, adding
a little more flour if needed to make a workable
dough.
Form into balls the size of large marbles and
cook in salted water kept at low boil until balls
rise to surface.
Makes about 25

## EGG DUMPLINGS

6 hard-cooked egg yolks
1/2 teaspoon flour
2 eggs, beaten
1 teaspoon salt
1/4 teaspoon pepper
1/2 teaspoon curry or nutmeg

Mash yolks and flour and mix in raw eggs and
seasonings, adding more flour to make a workable
dough.
Form into small balls or drop by half-teaspoonfuls
into gently boiling salted water. Cook 5 minutes or
until balls rise to surface.
Makes about 25

## BUTTER DUMPLINGS

1 egg, beaten
3-1/2 tablespoons softened butter
1/4 teaspoon salt
dash Lemon Celery*
dash paprika
dash thyme
1 teaspoon finely minced parsley
1/2 teaspoon finely minced chives
5-1/2 tablespoons flour

*see glossary

Mix egg, butter and seasonings. Stir in flour and let
stand at room temperature 1 hour.
Drop by teaspoonfuls into gently boiling salted
water or broth. They will be cooked when they rise
to the top.
Makes about 20

## EGG FOAM DUMPLINGS

1 egg white, beaten stiff

1 egg yolk, beaten
1/4 teaspoon salt
1/8 teaspoon nutmeg
1/8 teaspoon grated nutmeg
1 tablespoon each grated Parmesan cheese and
  fine bread crumbs

Combine yolk, seasonings, cheese and bread
crumbs. Gently fold into egg white and drop by
tablespoonfuls into well-seasoned stock kept at
slow boil. Simmer 5 minutes.
Makes about 12

## MARROW DUMPLINGS

2 3-inch marrow bones
1-1/2 tablespoons softened butter
1 egg
1 tablespoon minced parsley
6 tablespoons fine bread crumbs
1/4 teaspoon each salt and baking powder
1/8 teaspoon each black pepper and nutmeg

Push marrow from bones to make 3 tablespoons, mash with fork and mix in butter. Combine with rest of ingredients and form into small balls the size of a nutmeg.
Drop into gently boiling water and cook about 5 minutes until balls are slightly puffed and rise to top.
Be careful not to overcook.
Makes about 20 — extra good in tomato soup.

## BREAD DUMPLINGS

2 eggs, beaten
3/4 cup fine bread crumbs
1/2 teaspoon cornstarch
1 teaspoon milk
2 teaspoons finely minced parsley
1/2 teaspoon salt
1/2 teaspoon Lemon Onion*

* see glossary

Mix ingredients thoroughly and chill at least 1 hour. Form into 24 small balls and cook in simmering salted water 3 minutes after balls rise to the surface and puff up.

## ALMOND DUMPLINGS

1 cup finely crushed cracker crumbs
1/2 cup blanched almonds, ground coarsely
1/2 cup milk
1 beaten egg
3 tablespoons burnt butter
1 teaspoon salt
1/8 teaspoon white pepper
1/4 teaspoon Lemon Garlic*

flour

*see glossary

Mix ingredients, chill and form into small balls, using flour if needed to make a workable dough.
Drop into gently boiling salted water or stock; cook 5 minutes or until balls rise to surface.
Makes about 30

## MATZO DUMPLINGS

1/2 cup Matzo meal
1/2 cup well-drained, cooked chopped spinach
or 1/2 cup cooked ground pork, chicken, beef,
 liver, ham or turkey
or 1/4 cup grated cheese or ground cooked bacon
or combinations

Follow package directions for mixing Matzo balls. Use plain or add optional ingredients.
Follow package directions for cooking, but watch carefully — 20 minutes seems long enough.
Makes about 40

# CHOU DUMPLINGS

1/2 cup water
2 tablespoons butter
6 tablespoons flour
1 egg
1 tablespoon minced parsley
1/2 tablespoon minced chives
1/4 teaspoon salt
1/2 teaspoon celery salt or
Lemon Celery* or Lemon Dill*
1 tablespoon lemon juice
dash nutmeg

*see glossary

Bring water to boil with butter to melt butter. Add flour and stir vigorously until dough leaves side of saucepan. Cool slightly, beat in egg and rest of ingredients, mixing thoroughly.

Drop by teaspoonfuls into gently boiling salted water or directly into broth. Simmer until balls rise to top.

Makes about 25

## QUENELLES

1 cup ground poultry or game
1 egg, separated
2 tablespoons breadcrumbs
2 - 3 tablespoons poultry or game stock
1/4 teaspoon each salt, thyme, onion powder and
  Lemon Dill*
1/8 teaspoon white pepper
4 - 6 tablespoons lightly beaten egg white

*see glossary

Mix ground poultry or game, egg yolk, bread crumbs, stock and seasonings. Gently stir in egg white. Drop by teaspoonfuls into gently simmering salted water or broth and cook carefully 4 minutes or until slightly puffed.
Serve immediately.
Makes about 30 — very delicate!

## CHICKEN BALLS

1-1/2 cups ground, raw, white chicken meat
2 tablespoons finely minced parsley
1 egg, beaten
1/2 cup fine bread crumbs
1 tablespoon grated Romano cheese
1/4 teaspoon each salt and black pepper

Combine ingredients thoroughly, form into balls the size of large marbles and refrigerate several hours.
Cook in simmering salted water or stock 10 minutes.
Makes about 40 — may be frozen

## FORCEMEAT BALLS

1/2 cup ground cooked meat or poultry or game
2 hard-cooked egg yolks
1 teaspoon milk
3 tablespoons fine bread crumbs
1 beaten egg
1 teaspoon flour
1/4 teaspoon salt
1/8 teaspoon white pepper

Mash egg yolks with milk and mix with rest of ingredients. Flour hands and form small balls the size of a nutmeg. Drop into gently boiling water or broth and cook carefully until they rise to top.
Makes about 25
The broth should match the meat used in the balls.

## KOENIGSBERGER KLOPPS

1/4 pound each ground round steak and pork
1/8 pound ground veal
1/4 cup grated onion
1-1/2 tablespoons grated lemon peel
1 tablespoon lemon juice
2 slices white bread soaked in milk and
  squeezed dry
1 *small* egg
1/2 teaspoon salt
1/4 teaspoon black pepper

Combine ingredients thoroughly, form into balls the size of large marbles and refrigerate several hours.
Cook in simmering salted water or stock 10 minutes.
Makes about 40 — may be frozen

## CHIFFONADE

Sauté 1/2 cup chopped sorrel, spinach, lettuce or kale, or combinations in 2 tablespoons butter.

## FONDUE TOPPING

Heat 1/2 cup dry white wine in heavy saucepan or double boiler. Mix 1/2 cup shredded Gruyère cheese and 1/2 teaspoon cornstarch; gradually add to wine. Cook gently to melt and serve on hot soup.

## AIOLI SAUCE

Purée 2 - 4 minced garlic cloves, 1 egg yolk, 1/4 teaspoon salt and 1 teaspoon lemon juice in blender. Turn on high and in a steady stream add 2/3 cup olive oil. Adjust seasonings with salt and pepper.

## ROYALES

Simmer 1/2 cup rich stock with 1 minced garlic clove, 2 large sprigs parsley or chervil, and 1/8 teaspoon each savory and paprika for 10 minutes. Strain, cool and beat in 1 beaten egg and 1 beaten egg yolk. Sieve into buttered square pan and bake 20 - 30 minutes until knife inserted in center comes out clean. Cool, chill and cut into dice, or use small decorative cutters.
Or, after sieving, add 2 tablespoons of any ground cooked vegetable, meat, poultry, game, liver or bacon.

## CREAM, BROILED

Whip 1/2 cup heavy cream, add 2 tablespoons dry sherry, and spoon onto soup in 6 ovenproof bowls. Set 6 inches below heat and broil 1 minute. Watch carefully! Or whip 1/4 cup heavy cream and combine with 1/4 cup Hollandaise or mayonnaise.

## CREPES

Mix 1 egg, 1/2 egg shell of milk, 1 tablespoon flour and 1/8 teaspoon salt; add minced parsley or chives, if desired. Melt 1/8 teaspoon butter in 7-inch skillet, pour in half the batter, tip pan to coat bottom and brown. Turn and brown other side. Repeat with rest of batter. Roll, cut into strips, and garnish soup.

## GARNITURES

*Minced herbs and spices:* chives, dill, chervil, parsley, Italian parsley, Chinese parsley, rosemary, mint, fennel, green onions, celery leaves, watercress, lovage, borage, ginger, toasted poppy or sesame seeds, chopped sorrel.

*Blanched or browned vegetable dice or julienne:* celery root, beets, carrots, turnips, potatoes, artichoke hearts, asparagus tips, red onions, celery, green or red peppers, green beans, leeks, mushrooms, spinach.

*Uncooked vegetable dice or julienne:* radishes, red or green peppers, carrots, celery, avocados, tomatoes, mushrooms, cucumbers.

*Cooked poultry, game, meat dice or julienne*

*Citrus, sliced or wedged; grated peel, curls or tiny strips*

*Others:* popcorn, slivered toasted almonds, chopped, sliced or sieved hard-cooked eggs, sour cream with soy or paprika or caviar, heavy cream whipped with soy or paprika, grated cheeses, cheese balls, pork or bacon cracklings, sausages, rice, pastas, shellfish, olives, capers, pickles.

## CROUTONS

Dry in 200° oven sliced white, pumpernickel, rye, French or Italian bread cut into 1/2-inch squares. Toss 3 cups of croutons with 1/4 cup melted butter mixed with one of the following mixtures and brown in 300° oven, turning often.

1) 1/4 cup grated Parmesan, 1 teaspoon paprika, dash cayenne

2) 1/2 teaspoon salt, 1 - 2 teaspoons mixed herbs, pepper

3) 1-1/2 tablespoons lemon juice, 1 tablespoon grated lemon rind, 1 teaspoon paprika

4) 2 grated garlic cloves, 1/2 teaspoon oregano, salt, pepper

5) 1 teaspoon Lemon Dill* or Lemon Celery* seasoning

6) 1 teaspoon Cheesoning*

7) salt and cayenne pepper

8) 2 tablespoons grated Parmesan, 1 teaspoon paprika, 1/2 teaspoon garlic powder, 1/2 teaspoon onion juice

*see glossary

Bake in 275° oven, turning often, 1/2 - 1 hour until crisp and golden.

# Accompaniments

## SESAME WAFERS

Sift 1-3/4 cups sifted flour with 1 teaspoon garlic powder and 1/2 teaspoon salt. Cut in 1/2 cup butter until crumbly, stir in 1/2 cup sour cream lightly, using a fork to mix until *just* blended, and form into ball. Wrap in wax paper, chill several hours, roll 1/4-inch thick, cut into forms and place on cooky sheet. Brush with water and sprinkle with sesame seeds. Bake in 400° oven 15 minutes or until slightly puffed and golden.

## COCKTAIL RYE

Use slightly stale cocktail rye bread: 1) spread with melted butter, sprinkle with salt and caraway seeds, bake in 200°oven until crisp; 2) spread both sides with melted butter and bake crisp in 200° oven, turning several times; 3) spread with melted butter, sprinkle with grated Parmesan and bake in 200° oven until crisp.

## BREAD FINGERS, ROUNDS, SQUARES, TRIANGLES, RINGS

Use whole wheat, white, rye, French or Italian, paper-thin pumpernickel, slightly stale; spread with melted butter mixed with curry or poppy seeds or sesame seeds, or grated Parmesan and paprika. Bake in 200° oven until crisp.

182

## CORNUCOPIAS

Roll white bread, crusts removed, flat with rolling pin and spread with seasoned butter or any spread. Roll up from corner to corner, brush with melted butter and bake in 250° oven until golden, turning.

SPREADS: For 6 slices bread cut in rings, triangles or fingers, to be served with soup.

• Spread with 3 tablespoons butter, melted, beaten with 1 egg; roll in 1-1/2 cups freshly grated Parmesan cheese.

• Toast one side; spread untoasted side with herb butter: 1/2 cup soft butter blended with 2 teaspoons each chives and parsley, 1/4 teaspoon each basil, marjoram or oregano, and tarragon. Broil slowly.

• Melt 1/3 cup butter slowly with 2 pressed garlic cloves, 2 tablespoons Worcestershire sauce and 1/2 teaspoon salt. Spread on bread and bake in 200° oven 1 hour or until crisp and dry.

• Mushroom duxelle (see glossary) spread on untoasted side of bread and broiled. Make 1 cup for 6 pieces of bread.

## CREAM CHEESE PUFFS

3 ounces cream cheese, softened
1-1/2 teaspoons grated onion
1 egg yolk, beaten
1/4 teaspoon salt
1/8 teaspoon each white pepper and garlic powder
2 drops Tabasco
1/4 teaspoon Lemon Chef*

paprika
40 1-1/2-inch bread rounds or cocktail rye

*see glossary

Mix cheese, onion, egg yolk and seasonings; taste for salt.
Toast bread rounds on one side, spread untoasted side with cheese mixture and sprinkle with paprika.
Broil 5 inches from heat until puffy.

## CHEDDAR PUFFS

1/2 cup shredded sharp Cheddar cheese
1/4 cup finely minced red onion
1 teaspoon finely minced bell pepper
1/4 cup mayonnaise
2 drops Tabasco
1/8 teaspoon garlic powder

paprika
30 1-1/2-inch bread rounds or cocktail rye

Mix cheese, onion, bell pepper, mayonnaise, Tabasco and garlic powder; taste for salt.
Toast one side of bread rounds, spread untoasted side with cheese mixture and sprinkle with paprika.
Broil 5 inches from heat until golden and puffy.

## CHEESE SQUARES

1 egg, beaten
1 tablespoon flour
1/4 cup milk
1/3 cup grated Tybo or mozarella cheese
1/4 teaspoon salt
1/8 teaspoon black pepper
1/4 teaspoon Lemon Chef*

3 - 4 slices bread, crusts removed
3 - 4 tablespoons butter

*see glossary

Gradually beat flour into egg; blend in milk, cheese, and seasonings.
Dip bread slices into batter and sauté in butter until golden, turning once.
Cut into fourths.

# Glossary

*Aji Oil:* Chili oil; sesame oil with cayenne pepper.*

*Ala:* Bulgar small grain wheat. Available in grocery stores.

*Bean-Thread Noodles:* Also called peastarch, shining, cellophane and transparent noodles; opaque fine white noodle made from ground mung peas. Sold in long bundles by weight.*

*Boemboe Godok:* Mixed Indonesian spices, available in Mid-Eastern or Indonesian shops.

*Cheesoning:* A cheese-flavored seasoning put out by Reese. Available in grocery stores.

*Chinese Chives:* Flat-leafed chive with slight garlic flavor. Easily grown. Available in Oriental markets.

*File Powder:* Powdered sassafras leaves available in delicatessens and/or specialty shops.

*Fish Soy:* Fish sauce—water extract of fish with consistency of sesame oil.*

*Fungus, Black:* Also called cloud ear, brown fungus, tree fungus and wood ears. Irregularly shaped; expand 5 - 6 times original size and become gelatinous.*

*Goey Gaw:* Blown-up dried fish stomach; sold by weight.*

*Gobo:* Burdook root; long, thin brown root sold in Japanese markets.

*Hoisin Sauce:* Thick dark sauce of soy beans, chili, spices and garlic; in cans or bottles. Substitute soy and catsup.

*Hungarian Paprika:* Stronger than paprika; sold in most groceries. Available in bulk in Mid-Eastern shops.

*Jujubes:* Small dried red dates, slightly sweet. Sold by weight.*

*Kamaboko:* Steamed loaf made of fish forcemeat, dried and packaged.*

*Katsuobushi:* Dried bonito shavings sold by weight.*

*Kim Chee:* Pickled cabbage sold in jars, cans or bulk in Oriental markets. Can substitute sauerkraut.

*Kombu:* Dried sheet kelp for dashi.

*Laos:* Galangal powder, available in Mid-Eastern or Indonesian shops.

*Lemon Celery, Lemon Chef, Lemon Dill, Lemon Garlic, Lemon Herb, Lemon Onion:* Lemon seasonings adding distinctive flavor. Available in specialty shops, department store gourmet sections, and delicatessens. Or write:
  Shoffeitt Products Corp.
  Healdsburg, Calif. 95448

184

*Lop Chiang:* Chinese pork sausage available in Oriental markets freshly made or packaged.

*Lotus Root:* Water-lily root; tuberous stem of the water lily. Fresh in Oriental markets, or dried. Dried roots almost triple in size.*

*Matsutakefu:* Dried flavored wheat flour cakes packaged and sold by weight.*

*Mirin:* Japanese sweetish wine used in cooking; available in Japanese markets.

*Miso (Akamiso-red; shirumiso-white):* Fermented paste made of malt, salt and soy beans. Available in packages.*

*Mushroom Duxelle:* "Mushroom hash": sauté finely minced mushrooms to brown, add finely minced shallots, season to taste, sprinkle with flour, add cream to make thick mixture.

*Mushrooms, Forest:* Dried black (winter) mushrooms sold by weight.*

*Name-take: Tiny* mushrooms with stems; bottled.*

*Needles:* Also called golden needles, lily flowers or buds, lotus petals, or tiger lilies. Dried, highly nutritive; give off musky, sweetish flavor.*

*Oyster Sauce:* Thick oyster flavored sauce; should be available in grocery stores.*

*Oysters, Dried:* Small dried oysters with concentrated flavor. Sold by weight.*

*Pimentón:* Imported Spanish paprika similar in strength to Hungarian paprika. Available in bulk in Mexican or Spanish markets.

*Seaweed:* Dried kelp, bulk or sheets. Doubles in size when soaked. Bulk sold by weight; sheets in packages.*

*Serehpoeder:* Lemon grass powder, available in Mid-Eastern or Indonesian shops.

*Shichimi:* Japanese 7 seasoning pepper.*

*Shirataki Noodles:* Canned, thin yam-thread noodle available in Oriental markets.*

*Shrimp, Dried:* Tiny dried shrimp with concentrated flavor. Sold by weight.*

*Sour Salt:* Citric acid; available in groceries and specialty shops (French's).

*Tangerine Peel, Dried:* Dried tangerine, mandarin orange or orange peel; concentrated flavor. Sold by weight.*

*Tofu:* Bean curd, bean cakes *(not paste);* smooth, bland creamy custard made of puréed soybeans pressed into cakes. Instant available.*

*Tofu, Dried:* Bean curd pressed into thin, flat sheets and dried.*

*Turnip Greens, Dried:* Turnips and tops preserved with salt, dried and rolled.* Not to be confused with dried turnips.

*Available in Oriental markets. If unable to locate write P.O. Box 1074, San Rafael, Calif. 94901 for mail-order price list.

# Index

# About the Author

If one were to ask Coralie Davies Castle why cooking is so important to her, she would probably reply, "I guess it's just that I like to eat." But there are more complex reasons, too.

She claims to be a *hausfrau* from way back and recommends imaginative homemaking as an antidote to boredom and disillusionment with the outside world. She recalls spending hours as a small girl observing kitchen operations in her family's Kenilworth, Illinois, home, where she learned the tradition of German cookery.

However, it wasn't until she moved to Marin County, California, and started to explore San Francisco restaurants two and three times a week that food assumed its present importance in her life. After a year and nearly 200 restaurants, Mrs. Castle began trying to duplicate the recipes at home. She did not always succeed, but in the process of trying, she did develop delightful new dishes of her own. Encouraged by guests, family and friends she has seriously pursued cooking ever since, learning, originating, adapting, modifying and improving. Friends who have come to San Francisco from Indonesia, Brazil, Spain, Japan, Pakistan, Germany and other parts of the world added unusual ideas. Even her son contributed dishes from summers in Hawaii and Japan.

Second only to her kitchen is Coralie Castle's garden with its avocados, artichokes, seven kinds of citrus and a year-round supply of herbs and garnishes, as well as the usual fruits and vegetables. Ten years ago, Mrs. Castle assisted in establishing the Marin Community Workshop for Retarded and Handicapped Adults. It was her desire to help the workshop, along with her personal crusade to spur individual creativity, that led to this book. A share of her author's royalties have gone to help meet the Workshop's urgent needs.